Selected Poems

SELECTED POEMS

by

SACHEVERELL SITWELL

with a Preface by OSBERT SITWELL

GERALD DUCKWORTH & CO. LTD.
3 HENRIETTA STREET, LONDON, W.C.2

Collected Poems *first published* 1936
This Selection first published 1948

All rights reserved

To
BRYHER

*Printed in Great Britain by
Billing and Sons Ltd., Guildford and Esher*
F8680

PREFACE

By Osbert Sitwell

THERE are those, I apprehend, who find enthusiasm in one member of a family for the gifts of another, offensive. Let me avow in reply that, though not by nature of an excessive modesty, have I not a thousand times longed to have been endowed with a hundredth part of my brother's creative power and sensibility, and that, moreover, I have in countless instances been inspired to write by the reading of his poems! It would be therefore stupid of me, as well as ungrateful, to pretend that I prefer to them the work of other and lesser poets who happen not to be related to me. But, in fact, it may be the gifts and not the mutual enthusiasm, to which objection is taken? In that case let us hope that those who make moan will be spared similar affliction for as long as divides us in space of time from any like emergence in the past. . . No, in approaching Mr. Sacheverell Sitwell's poems, I have been guided, not by fraternal partiality, but, I acknowledge, by bias; an undoubted prejudice in favour of any remarkable contemporary work that comes my way. And even those who may hold that a brother should not write a preface, will agree that on two scores at least I am well qualified to judge Mr. Sacheverell Sitwell's poems; I have been privileged to watch in every phase his development, and I know better than most the respects in which he differs in aim and execution from his brother and sister.

The selection which follows, and which has been made

by Miss Edith Sitwell and myself, may not be ideal, but will prove, I hope, useful. The rigours of current conditions in publishing have compelled us to cut long passages and, indeed, remove several whole poems which ought to have been included. (For example, we have been obliged to omit in its entirety the amazing *Dr. Donne and Gargantua:* because it is an extremely long poem, forming indeed a volume by itself, and we found it impossible to separate any portion of it from the context.) We have, however, tried to give examples of each vein and phase of Mr. Sitwell's poetic genus at its finest and most typical, so that a new reader, even turning a page, will not have to ask in what the peculiar gifts of the poet consist.

As to the virtues of this poet, I claim for him a prodigious vigour of thought, of imagery and rhythm, a temperamental fire, and an ability to produce a sense of prodigality and profusion in a dingy screwpenny age of pinched and withered talents, a boldness and largeness that set him apart from most of his contemporaries. No poet of his time has been similarly equipped to face his task. The forfeit he pays is that the very wealth of his invention tends on occasion to dwarf the immense scale of his work : or at times to lead him to descend into lesser lands, or to stray for a moment into others just because he has newly created them. His Pegasus is unduly impatient and wasteful, and quickly abandons pastures which would have furnished another with material for a whole career. . . . Yet what an extraordinary power this poet shows in every line : what a capacity to carry his readers impetuously along, draw them into his own globes of fire and air, and point out to them the paths which lead into the sacred woods : and, in an opposite direction, what a true and delicious lyricism he manifests. His gifts, nevertheless, are difficult to define. He is a poet of fire, but not of the hearth, a poet of nature, but not of the shires (of what by this I intend to signify, I shall have more to say in a moment), a poet who creates myths, and yet is a realist, intensely modern, intensely informed and civilised, yet one who has preserved a primitive or Greek approach to natural objects, to homely flowers and sights, albeit he turns with ease to create towering images, and to tell us of whole lost worlds, of fantastic cities and the most tragic epochs. About his genius and career there is an element of paradox—though that is particularly absent from his books. The least controversial of writers (in all probability there is more of paradox and provocation in the foregoing six hundred words, than in the whole enormous body of his work), he has often found himself engaged in bitter controversy. And, again, though still under fifty years of age, he has been for thirty years a famous writer, with a name familiar to all authors in Europe and America; and, while in the consideration of poets, he has long been one of the most highly rated of the living, yet even now his poems have not enjoyed the same wide fame as his prose books have earned him. It may be, therefore, that this selection will bring to his poetry a fresh band of enthusiasts.

To them it may come as a shock—as I confess it did to me at the time these poems were composed—to realise that the first *Serenade,* the mysteriously warm and evocative *Tahiti,* and the epigrammatic *Psittacus,* and other as exquisite and original work, had been written by a boy under twenty. Since then, he has lighted for us many lamps—

but how inadequate a phrase is this!—has caused, rather, many great fires of the mind to reveal in an ecstasy of light forgotten moments, full of an unimaginable significance! He has given us such books as *Southern Baroque Art*, unique work of critical and poetic appreciation, *The Dance of the Quick and the Dead*, and *The Hunters and the Hunted*, but these early poems to which I have referred, though they lack the imaginative heights and physical energy later to be displayed in the *Battle of the Centaurs*, and albeit they do not offer us the age-old, vibrant immensity of *Agamemnon's Tomb*—to me, among the greatest of modern poems—yet manifest a youthful ingenuousness and ingenuity that are most deeply moving. Nor has his sense of character—though it is evinced in several later books—been often better displayed in his poetry than in *Week Ends*, that brief, delicious, musical dialogue between a commanding woman and the gardener, pitched in a privileged sea-side pleasaunce for elderly ladies and their Aberdeen terriers, set back behind the green spears of railings, now in all probability melted down, like the conventions that gave birth to them. Surely if he had chosen, Mr. Sitwell might have made a memorable novelist, for this comparatively short poem is an epitome of the lost civilisation I endeavoured to present in *Before The Bombardment*. Nevertheless, though when once the howls of "Cad!" raised in certain quarters on the publication of my first novel had died down, this book soon earned a wide and appreciative public, I find readers have been slow to relate it to *Week Ends* and other early poems of my brother's, which, in addition to my own youthful observation, perhaps prompted me to undertake that work.

Some readers may, furthermore, find the interplay of ideas among three writers who were so closely related, yet subsequently to develop along such different lines, of some interest. My brother, the youngest of us, was necessarily influenced by voices that had not existed in the formative years of my sister and myself. It is one of the paradoxes of art that not seldom a lesser poet or painter influences a greater for his good, and the impact of the poems of Marinetti, the founder of the Italian Futurists, upon my brother, who first read him at sixteen years of age, can be detected in these earlier poems. Indeed there is in Sacheverell Sitwell a union of Italian inspiration and fertility with northern vigour which rendered him very liable to Latin influences.

In this connection, something remains to be said. It has, I understand, been objected by certain austere persons, that there exists in his work a deliberate exoticism; that he was not so much concerned, for instance, with the Spanish Civil War—that most dreary and dunder-headed beano for international left-wing journalistic busybodies, that battle of crooks, leading brave men to destruction over the prostrate body of a nation—as with the Battle of the Centaurs. Well, similarly, I suppose, Milton should have dealt with the squalid contemporary conflict between Cavalier and Roundhead instead of writing of that between the angelic hosts. In addition, it must be remembered that my brother knew Spain too well to wish to take sides or to feel anything but misery at the plight of a noble and magnificent people. In somewhat the same fashion, he has been censured for writing of orange trees rather than hazel nuts, and of the vine, rather than the more homely hop or potato

—a criticism singularly inept, for what other modern English poet has so impressively celebrated the common English fruit trees as has he in *Hortus Conclusus!* The truth is, of course, that to him, the orange tree was almost as early and frequent a recollection as apple or pear (to which fortunate fact we owe two of the most beautiful of his lesser poems, *Orange Tree by Day* and *Orange Tree by Night*), and that he was only eleven years of age when my father bought an Italian home. Moreover, I still recollect with intense pleasure from years even previous to that the long journeys we took together to Italy, when I was eleven and twelve, and my brother six, when Europe was still unscarred by modern warfare, and all European lands were one, and where every town we passed on the way was full of a promise of an infinite enchantment. Italy was bountiful with her gifts to my brother, as she has been to many English writers before him: and some of these poems are no less the fruit of it, than others are of his English blood, upbringing and environment. It is partly this which enabled him to be a writer of the world as well as of one country.

OSBERT SITWELL.

CONTENTS

PREFACE BY OSBERT SITWELL - - - - - - v

GROUP I

	PAGE
Rio Grande and Four Poems from *The Santander Quartet*	15
In the Wine Shop	17
Telling Fortunes	18
At Supper	20
Gypsy Song	21

GROUP II

Two Variations on Themes out of *Zarathustra*	23
"Laughing Lions will Come"	23
Parade Virtues for a Dying Gladiator	29

GROUP III

Et in Arcadia Omnes. (Extract from *The Bird-Actors*) - 37

GROUP IV

Actor Rehearsing - - - - - - - 47

GROUP V

Fisherman	67
Wind as Husbandman	68

GROUP VI

From *Canons of Giant Art: Twenty Torsos in Heroic Landscapes*	71
Fugal Siege	71
Pastoral	78
Agamemnon's Tomb	85
From *Battle of the Centaurs*. (Centaurs and Lapithæ)	94
The Farnese Hercules	100
Fragment from *Bohemund, Prince of Antioch*	108

GROUP VII

	PAGE
The People's Palace	113
Trumpets	113
Outskirts	114
"Psittacus Eois Imitatrix Ales ab Indis." (Ovid)	116
Pindar	117
Brighton Pier	119
Li-Tai-Pé	120
The Moon	121
Tahiti	121
Barrel Organs	123
Mrs. H. or a Lady from Babel	126
Week Ends	128
Valse Estudiantina	131

GROUP VIII

Extracts from *The Thirteenth Cæsar*	135
The Opening of the Tomb	135
At the Bedside	135
As of Old	138

GROUP IX

Serenades	141
Sigh soft, sigh softly	141
Open your window. Let the air flow in	141
I see no breath upon the window's water	142
Hortus Conclusus	143
Cherry Tree	143
Gardener's Song	144
The Red-Gold Rain	145
i. Orange Tree by Day	145
ii. Orange Tree by Night	146
Damson and Medlar	146
Dandelion	148
Cowslips	148
Variation on a Theme by Robert Herrick	149

CONTENTS

	PAGE
Complaint	149
Warning	150
The Island	152
Derbyshire Bluebells	152
Fortune	155
Shadow	156

GROUP X

A March Past at the Pyramids - 159

GROUP XI

Two Mirror Poems - 169
    On a Name Scratched upon a Window - 169
    The Poet and the Mirror - 170

GROUP XII

Part II from *New Water Music* - 173

GROUP XIII

Studies on the Black Keys - 179
    The Dark of Night - 179
    Black Sonnet - 180
    Black Shepherdess - 180
Two Pastoral Poems - 181
    The Cyder Feast - 181
    Chamber Idyll - 183

GROUP XIV

White Rose - 187
The Mezquita - 188
The Lime Avenue - 188
Outside Dunsandle - 189
The Sick Man - 189

INDEX OF FIRST LINES - 191

ACKNOWLEDGEMENT

The poems in Group VI (*Canons of Giant Art*) were first published by Faber and Faber, Ltd., those in Group VII (*The People's Palace*) by Basil Blackwell: both of whom have kindly given permission for them to be reprinted in this volume.

GROUP I

Rio Grande and Four Poems from The Santander Quartet

The Rio Grande

By the Rio Grande
They dance no sarabande
On level banks like lawns above the glassy, lolling tide;
Nor sing they forlorn madrigals
Whose sad note stirs the sleeping gales
Till they wake among the trees, and shake the boughs,
And fright the nightingales;
But they dance in the city, down the public squares,
On the marble pavers with each colour laid in shares,
At the open church doors loud with light within,
At the bell's huge tolling,
By the river music, gurgling, thin,
Through the soft Brazilian air.

The Comendador and Alguacil are there
On horseback, hid with feathers, loud and shrill
Blowing orders on their trumpets like a bird's sharp bill
Through boughs, like a bitter wind, calling;
They shine like steady starlight while those other sparks are falling
In burnished armour, with their plumes of fire,
Tireless, while all others tire.
The noisy streets are empty and hushed is the town
To where, in the square, they dance and the band is playing

Such a space of silence through the town to the river
That the water murmurs loud
Above the band and crowd together;
And the strains of the sarabande,
More lively than a madrigal,
Go hand in hand
Like the river and its waterfall
As the great Rio Grande rolls down to the sea.
Loud is the marimba's note
Above these half-salt waves,
And louder still the tympanum,
The plectrum, and the kettledrum,
Sullen and menacing
Do these brazen voices ring.
They ride outside,
Above the salt sea's tide,
Till the ships at anchor there
Hear this enchantment
Of the soft Brazilian air,
By those Southern winds wafted,
Slow and gentle,
Their fierceness tempered
By the air that flows between.

The Santander Quartet in a Programme of Spanish Music

In the Wine-Shop

TALL as a ghost . . . outside . . . the soldier :
Like a Gibbet . . . the shadow made by his gun :
He is waiting to shoot me
Till moon goes out and the shadows run :
He will shoot me from the battlements
As I get to the sea,
I shall stumble on the sand
And a wave will cover me.
My trousers flap in the wind
As I stand at the door,
Like a white sail they will warn him,
He will hear my feet on the floor.
I will push my mask up
And sniff the sky.
I will sit on a barrel,
Quiet and shy :
But he never stirs
And he never looks inside,
So I'll cross to the counter
And need not hide.
My glass fills red with the wine
And new blood runs in my veins;
If I go to the soldier now,
Like a horse without bit, without reins,
Will I make his life gallop away from him,
Till his heart . . . those thundering hoofs, . . . stops dead :

I will lift his arms and let them fall,
He moves not his hands nor his head.
Quicker than thought have I killed him,
But still he is standing outside;
Unless I drink wine and have courage
I shall never set sail this tide.
So I called for more, but as I drank
The moon leaned on the window sill
As though to climb in like a lover;
Down I pulled my pointed bill,
To mask me so he could not know:
Across the shadow to the door I crept,
I heard his breath and turned the latch
And choked him, so they thought I wept:
None of them looked out through the glass,
None of them saw the moon's cold stare,
But I ran, breaking through its beams,
Although I heard the trumpet's scare
Blown from the battlements shrill and loud,
I crept on down the wall's black shade,
While up above like cocks they crowed
And drowned the noise my moving made;
So loud, they even mute my oars
And let me row out in the boat
Until I climb the hempen ladder
Whose rope should noose my neck and throat.

Telling Fortunes

SHAKE, stone shades,
Beneath my cornet:
I buzz like rattled glass
And sting like a hornet.

Come into the shadow's
Dry, stony meadow:
This is the Gypsy's tent,
No roof, no rent.
My yellow corn,
Those stars that spark,
Stab like a blown horn.
Run not, ragged wind;
Lie by me,
Like my dog who lies beside me!
Blow on the flames, hush down the dark,
Make hot for me, my cooking pot.
Water's thin mind,
Smoke, or steam,
Shapes your dread,
Or shows your dream.

Stand in the tent door,
Rich and poor:
While my soup stews,
Gold, or iron,
Sun, or dews,
Lamb, or lion;
This broth I brew
Tells truth to you.
My gold corn fades,
The stars die down,
Up creep the shades
And leave the town.
My field I pitched on
Lifts from me:
Cool are my embers
In this mist.
No one remembers,

The thin forms twist,
Worse ghosts are these
Than those I raised:
I'll sound in the trees
And make them dazed.
Hear my cornet, boughs and branches,
The winds, those ice cold avalanches,
Cannot damp my trumpet breath,
It comes on iron feet, breathing death.

At Supper

Bread, cheese and wine.
We'll bring our chairs and dine
Where the cruel lights whine,
Or purr from their doors
Like murmurs off the golden shores
Where the circus animals, stretched upon the sand,
Sleep in the yellow light they never understand.
The lion:

> " Why do these bars not turn to gold?
> I would leap through sunlight out of my black lair
> Breaking the sun's gold hair
> That binds me;
> But this dreadful bar reminds me
> How my mane, like sun's hot crest,
> Waved on the wind:
> Now I'm caged and have no rest,
> No peace of mind."

The seal in a soft sleep dreams: "Am I
Swimming again where the salt waves sigh:
Those circus lights that groan always
Changed to cold seas on snowy days?"
The bull:

"My mother lows once more for me
In this field that lies before me
Covered with young grass to crop:
But when I reach for it, I drop:
This bitter sand, so cruel, so salt,
My pasture—though I've done no fault."

Gypsy Song

WIND barked all night just outside
Worrying the tent wall at my side,
Then a cock crowed through the whining
And, next, the winter sun was shining:
Half my day I live this way.

The roads are windy corridors
Cold from the clouds those matadors
That will not let the red sun out;
And so through cold I crawl about,
Hunting, begging, all the day.

Fire, fierce animal that warms me,
If I'm careful never harms me:
I have no time for it till night,
No fire, by day, but sun's white light,
And he'll not answer, when I pray.

GROUP II

Two Variations on Themes out of Zarathustra

"Laughing Lions will Come" (*Nietzsche*)

THE prophet from his desert cave
   Listens to the sound of water
Lapping with tongues the fringes of the sand.
   Young flowers open for the bees;
   A roadway for the yellow sun
   Climbs from the hills into the fallow sea.
The scented bells hold golden sound
And the strong lion drinks the salted waves,
Cooling his mane within the sudden foam.
   The bee skirts tremblingly the shining dew,
   Looking for honey in the golden dells,
   While the lion shakes the loud hills again.
This early morning there may lie some gold
Forgotten when the light was fled;
To-day the great beams may shine
   On opened caves where run swift rivers
   Shooting their arrows at the swordless sea,
   And blind to the sun whose shining armour
Shows in the sky among the clouds he charges,
Driving them across a wind walled field
Into the shelter of the towering hills.

Honey may be hiding in the waking flowers:
The man in armour hides behind the gold:
The strongest waves, far off, are snow.
These are dangers to the daring robber,
The armoured impotence of man made deity,
And crowd thick, barking heads, on the lionlike sand.
  Gathering honey in the rolling desert,
  Such are the perils to a fasting prophet—
  Doglike men, and menlike gods.
Many doors lie open into his cave,
For lion springs, flash of the surging sea,
And dogs that bark to bar him from his palm.
  To leave his cave, and walk on the burning sand,
  He passes the sun that bridles his yellow mane,
  And the roaring crowd, an ocean of clashing waves.
Tight rope dancers run over the roofs
And fall in the market-place—
Raising a laugh,
  It looks like walking on the rainbow's bridge
  Among the clouds, behind the windows;
  There, below, fly the flags of smoke
Waving possession that the Lord's at home
And works, a creator, in his own fair garden
Where trees spring as fountains, lift into the air,
  Their branches steadied in the height with wings
  That quiver in the stream of wind,
  And by the cold are frozen as they drop,
Before they foam again as fiery darts
Piercing the soft breasts of the pool,
They tremble above the water, birdlike, with flashing feathers.
  Is Zarathustra armoured that he goes
  Leaving his cave, down mountains,
  Fording swift rivers, to attain the town?

The tight rope dancers had turned back again,
Waving their wands to balance a sharp curve,
They stagger as a child who learns his walk
   Using a crutch in place of human hand,
   Holding his own high above the head
   To guide him on an easy, level path—
Guitars are played by men upon high stilts
Stepping over gardens to keep up the tune
Because the dancers only move with music;
   With creaking leg and hollow tread
   They walk among the houses, chase the rope,
   And whisper warning while they play more loud.
Below, the cripples lean out from their corners;
And a dwarf or two will strain his little stride
To run like a child holding a strong kite.
   This is the magnet drawing every eye
   When Zarathustra comes behind the curtain of the gold
      horizon,
   Walks into the town through the deserted gates.
Judges are holding back the wheel of time,
Fitting the spokes to figures on a watch
As they follow the competitors on airy paths.
   He walks beneath an archway, hears his tread,
   Multiplied and echoed in this empty hall,
   And then is alone again on empty street.
Stepping out firm, he starts to sing,
Turns the corner and is in the square,
His song a loud river that now joins the sea.
   Who will he first step up to,
   Take by the shoulder,
   To break down his stare?
Will he stoop down to a dwarf and shout,
Ask him to run across the square
And beg the Mayor to stop festivities a moment?

Is it too dangerous to hold a stilt
Shouting out loud into the noisy air
To attract attention from a wooden giant?
If he holds a stilt and stops the music
Down will tumble all the tight rope dancers,
And the men who play the mandolines cannot stand still.
    Shout as loud as he possibly can,
    He will never drown the music
    And the roaring crowds.
One course, one only, is there to his hand;
Wonder and marvel are the joys today,
And this is the course that he must tread.
    God goes on a cloud,
    But the dancers walk there,
    And the crowd shout louder than the singing of His
      angels.
Thinking a moment, Zarathustra stopped,
Stroked his beard, and hesitated
Till his mind lit up;
    Without a cry, without a word,
    He started running down the square,
    Raced ever quicker till he reached a wall;
No sooner touched it,
Than he turned again,
Running ever faster than the way he came;
    Reached the starting point,
    Turned once more,
    Raising a dust to hide his face.
The men on stilts looked down like birds
Who watch for prey in the glistening grass,
And dropped the instruments from their hands;
    The dancers when the music stopped
    Swayed on their ropes
    And fell like stars,

Flashed through the air with trailing sparks
And opened on the ground
Their clumsy petals.
　　The dwarfs and cripples raised themselves,
　　Came from their corners into dazzling sun
　　And ran among the crowd to start them running.
Soon Zarathustra showed in front,
Just behind were the men on stilts,
After them the able bodied ran,
　　Followed by cripples and the bounding dwarfs;
　　Half of them are running from right to left,
　　While Zarathustra showed from left to right.
Soon he caught the laggards and the limping halt
And ran among their crutches
By the jumping dwarfs.
　　This time, turning down a narrow street,
　　He ran into a house
　　And climbed the shaking stairs;
Out from the window on a roof he stepped
While the people ran up stairways
Like a flood inside a well;
　　Down a drainpipe on the ground again
　　He heard the tumbling ceilings
　　And the roofs fall in.
While the survivors took the road again
Zarathustra ran out from a gate once more
Till he reached the burning sand,
　　And fell back breathless,
　　Blind from the dust
　　And dead with running.
Clouds of dust still rose from the town,
Blurred murmurs,
And the tread of hundreds running.

"I won attention by my ruse.
Shouting was vain, and had I showed
Floating above them on a cloud
They would have guessed me lowered from a tower,
Treading the yielding clouds like a man through snow,
So I had to run among them like a wind;
But for all my running they have never seen
The stride of my footsteps,
But thought themselves
Each in each other to contain the cause.
My years of meditation in a cave
Gave more hope for another visit,
But now that they run themselves around the town
Nothing will stop them but themselves alone.
If someone with young lungs
Blew out through a trumpet the last chance for man,
It would be a feature in their entertainment.
I must look at the sun,
Who sinks to die
And pours his treasures to the sea to keep,
Guarding them with tempests and a change of tide;
So that in sinking to the sunless caves,
Where they lie to light the darkness till he comes again,
The poorest fisherman has golden oars
To row with over the echoing waves,
Suddenly shaking their yellow manes
To sound new music to the gods below;
And when the gold is taken from the oars
The music ceases and the waves are mute
Till a new wind whispers from the thirsty trees
And the fisherman can hoist his sail."

Parade Virtues for a Dying Gladiator

For safety, hear this, common mortals!
March with the others—swing your arms—
Don't step too fast—don't reach so far.
. . . Laggards are devoured by wolves:
If you but reach the enemy first
An eagle from the iron air
Will soar steep down, and peck your eyes.
Be the first to steal down fire
And you shall lie on the aching rock,
A threatening wing your roof and shade.

The scaffold stands and totters in the wind,
A cage for the light—a platform through the clouds:
Remark—a scaffold and a scaffolding,
A terrace for death—and bars for young birds.

At the top he stoops to work,
The shadows give him longer limbs,
He strides on stilts to tie the ropes,
Only string can hold the floors
And keep the telescopic roofs apart.
A little rubbing of dry hands,
Snatches of sawdust on the floor,
Then he nods for the fanfare like a God.

A screech of trumpets—before we guess,
Before we know what he stands there for,
The planks split up, they bend like rushes,
The frightened birds fly off, he tumbles,
Falls through the brittle lights that snap
And give like waves when a meteor falls;

Now he crumples on the sand,
Let him collect himself, spit blood and words.

They flood the arena—cover the sands—
The beakèd war boats raise their sails,
Like birds they tack in the wind.

The second philosopher appeared,
Proudly holding a ladder.
" Wait," he was saying, " till we're near enough,
Then watch me making for another world."
He did not climb. He lined the deck,
The sailors helped him, charged with their ram,
The other ship was staggered, helpless.
They lay alongside, near enough,
Over with the ladder, he climbed along.
His little weight decided things,
The two boats went apart, the hooks,
The claws of his ladder were wrenched out,
He lay like a man between wild horses.
One arm came off, and then a leg.
They picked him into a boat, rowed off,
Drained out the water, and when the sand was dry,
There he lay close to the other,
The two philosophers together again.

The third put up a horn to his mouth.
" I deny," he roared, " a better world,
But I hope a stranger, not a nicer heaven.
Also your fault—and not my choice."
And then he disappointed the crowd,
Fell, like a log, without one struggle,
Killed by poison, drunk in secret.

PARADE VIRTUES FOR A DYING GLADIATOR

"As my turn," the fourth man shouted,
"I'll walk on stilts through the drying water,
Collect the bodies, carry them out,
And give them to the crowd for burial."
Then he began tremendous tests,
Beat one stilt with an axe to break it,
Looked through the eyeholes of his visor,
Bared an arm to feel his sword.
Then on one leg his whole weight leaning,
He strapped his other leg to the stilt,
Knocking it on to a wall to test it;
Both legs finished, he cannot stand,
He has to stamp and stagger around,
A tireless peripatetic.
They hand him helmet, sword, and trident,
And, last of all, the trumpet that he hollo's down.
Now he is ready to start, steel clad,
And shod with hoofs of sounding wood.
He grips the trumpet with his teeth,
Bares the trident, holds the net.
The first he comes to still is breathing.
He lances him with the trident, lifts him,
Opens the net for the crumpled body.
The second man, legless, armless,
Lies there helpless.
Little is left for the wide tongued trident.

The man who drank the poison died,
But still the venom lives within him.
He is spiked with the same three lances,
And the same points transfixing both,
Killed the other who was breathing,
But being limbless could not move.
The weight of the two together stifled,

Strained, and made this gladiator gasp—
To right himself, he must stand still,
He stumbled, drew to his height,
And fell.

Next we saw one stilt come out,
And wave above the shallow water.
He disengaged it, dropped it off,
The other leg was doubled up,
But he could sit kneedeep in water,
And use the floating stilt as a crutch.
His trident stuck up out of the sand,
The visor and the trumpet still were his:
Helmet for head, and tube for voice,
Enough material for martial music.
The drums were rattling for his death,
But there he sat, and did not die.
He had the only pair of stilts,
And whilst the water ebbed from him,
Leaving this monster on the sand,
He can string out platitudes,
And make a dying actor's speech.

" How do we differ from dull soldiers?"
These were the words he started with.
" Where is the gulf for us to jump,
Where are the stairs for me to climb,
So that I ride a horse, a cloud,
And rule the azure fields of air?
Why do I want these: is it vain
To try and open gates of glass?
They are transparent, is it vanity
That I wish for men to see me
Ride beneath these gates, and glitter,

Shine the other side from them?
Now they stand, where there I stood,
They see me where I nothing saw,
But when I came behind the glass,
The light to show me, dazzled me,
Now I grope through a golden fog,
I stumble on the beams as stones,
I never see the road I walked:
Lamps blind me; blatant shouting deafens me:
The more I stumble, more they cheer.

I suggest these virtues to all dying gladiators.
Never bury your rivals' bodies, let their corpses taint the air,
Do not put them in caves for the relic hunters,
But leave them to the vultures, they will quicken the decay.
This virtue I learnt, first, today.
Your enemies must feel both edges of the sword;
They shall be laggards for all hungry wolves;
And prey for the vultures if they die too soon:
This is why I build my house
Using tombstones from damp fields,
That is why I said today
I'd gather the bodies and give them to you,
Letting you dig and hide them for yourselves,
And keep you busy, fill your minds,
So that while I stand in the glare
You watch me not, but grope with your hands,
Running the sand through greedy fingers.

Now I have light more prying than the sun,
No audience so nervous as the fainting stars
Who gently withdraw, but watch behind the dark;
None are there, spying.
   So you see I have gathered my rivals,

Given them over to you, occupied your attention,
Now there is full light for me, and no rivalry,
Alone I can work my wonders, alone in my own hours of
    day."
  But then he worked his own greatest wonder,
  His head dropped, knees sank, and he rolled into the
    water.

That is a virtue, but not a parade one:
Soldiers should run away to live another day.
Good as far as he went.
Good to gather and expose the corpses,
But weak of him to die, kneedeep in water.
I should admire him more, sitting on his box
Or washed ashore on a querulous hencoop.
This much I like, that he walked on stilts,
That the rôle he chose never let him stop,
That he could not stand, but must stamp ahead.

It seemed to me, if my turn should come,
That I would not take the sand, scour out,
And clear the threshold of the statue dust;
Any more than build with the dead, mute, stone;
That I would not snap the fallen swords,
Or sharpen their points to help me,
Neither slay the old, nor build the new religion,
Neither beg the streets, nor live on an altar.

Parade these virtues, dying gladiators!
Beware of the final, finishing copestone.
Hang many masks from your belt,
But the last one awkwardly stops your disguise,
Until you break the string, to take the bead—
And tumble the walls of your Paradise.

If you cage your growing trees,
No birds will float through them and sing;
If there are walls, you cannot watch
The fields that slope down till they hold the deep sea.
Between yourself and the waves there lie
All that divides and walls you in.
A Paradise is dangerous to hunt through
For the rare tigers among the tropical trees;
If you had never attempted this,
You had never been lying wounded now.

An icy wind interrupted this flow,
A fall of stage snow fluttered from the roof,
We were aghast to see the gladiator
Rolling the snow in his trembling hands—
Not to soothe him—for the next scene was a fight on sledges—
But the gladiator finished several handfuls
And then he threw them into the audience.
It was a very irritating dust,
And broke in clouds, till everybody sneezed.
So I took my hat and coat and went,
Letting them sneeze and seeing them weep—
And I turned this thought in my mind.
Surely the gladiator threw this snow
Wanting their tears for two good reasons:
" First," said he, " I'll have them cry,
Their tears shall flow for my timely death;
Secondly, their tears shall hide and veil
Until with smarting they cannot see:
And then they'll miss my proud successor."

GROUP III

Et in Arcadia Omnes
(Extract from *The Bird-Actors*)

THE stars, but prophets call them sons of God,
   Lay in the fresh field, and the cool wind trod,
Striding, across the bodies where they slept
And woke them to the glory that they kept
All day in bondage until darkness came,
When movement flowed as water, gold as flame.

The gods now rise and let the new light run,
Rippling its quick strong life and substance spun
From fluttering wings and fiery breasts of clouds
Along their limbs just risen from the shrouds
Of deathlike slumber, till they play again;
Blue hills, far islands watch them, and the plain.

Above white clouds the stars come from their tent
On which today's dead light spills lustre, spent
And feeble after fiery beams and bars
Have burned the sea with madness, earth with wars,
And made still waters mirror in their glass
The gold hung woods, and gliding clouds that pass,
Dip their tall towers like pennons in the lake
When, hidden from the sun, their thirst they slake
Till, at the time the nightingales begin,
The clouds have vanished, and the night is thin.

Now at their settled stations in the sky
The stars are still, or spread their wings to fly,
Are motionless, or moving with their gold
Through Heavens wide as water, and as cold.
Looking between sharp edges of the leaves
Beneath black shadowed houses, and their eaves
Still shining in the evening rain, there show
Unfolding flowers that tremble as they grow,
And several ships with glittering sails of glass
Swim the blue seas, or float beneath the mass
Of towering cliffs down which the gold men leap,
Cross the wide sands, run down the shelving steep,
Ride on the foam, and climb the golden ropes
Until the soft breathed wind fulfil their hopes.

Now that the sky is once more set with signs,
From balconies above a tree that shines
With fanlike agitation of the wind
Revolving its lush petals till they bind
Their spinning dance into a formless round,
The people lean and listen to the sound
Of voices parting the dim green, and strings
That wavelike beat their foam upon the wings
Flashing below the crystal fall of song,
Which, melting, drops in music on the throng;
From bird throats kissing the warm air there drops
The mingling of cool snow and flame through stops
Of flutelike tongues that gather fire from light
To make their honey golden to our sight.

The poorest, even, have their hour of pleasure
When the daylight fails
And the more advanced young women
Play the piano,

While the more advanced young men
Accompany them with song,
And those who cannot play their part,
Sit in the window.

At a late hour all the voices stop,
The day's perpetual sound is dead:
So still now
That you think the singers
Must still be in the room,
The women sleeping with the half-closed eyes
Of waxwork figures,
And the men as plaster caryatids
Upholding the low roofs of lodging houses
On their sad, crushed heads.
The next few hours are far the best
In which to temper truth with a trite compromise.

In more imaginative lands
Our instruments are still the strings
That carry every trembling confidence
Through a half-open window—
Till, stepping to the water's edge,
You see your own tall shadow
In the clear windows of the water
With white pointed mask
Abetting your new self disguised;—
And all the music of the air obeys
The silver presence singing in the trees
And giving time its intervals of lucid silence,
While wind touches the taut strings of the sea,
And the waterfalls of light
Drip through the leaves
Upon the dew drenched grass.

If such and such sit in the gamut of one's life,
Within the same close box of yellow bricks,
Under a mutual roof;
Bow from the windows if you walk beneath
And leash themselves to let you climb the stairs,
Is not a little latitude allowed
For subtle insolence, and half-veiled threats?

Calling through the lattices of leaves
At those wreathed windows
Where, flowerlike, the gold light hangs,
Wise birds repeat,
As echoes from cool caves,
The words they're taught.

A wall of cactus guards the virgin sound
Of piano scales
Ringing the changes
In a small schoolroom,
And on the black keys
Hammering with the hard beak of woodpeckers
On a moss grown tree.
From all around young ardent voices
Reiterate the aged sentiments,
While a brave few try the spiral stairs,
Spinning like blown smoke to the glittering stars,
Half-lost in the damp breath of clouds
That tarnish the gilt edges of their song.

Through the splintered stillness
Sounds like small animals
Creep from their holes,
And from a hundred various heights,
From terraces of all the shaking fields of leaves,

The frail ladders
On which our meaning climbs
Span the blue air
Until they touch the sodden ground.

Music, that on the stooping sails of wind,
Drifting, divides the distance, and can bind
Those it has chosen with a supple string,
Keeping them motionless to feel her wing,
Can negative the constant turn of time
And make long minutes shorter than the chime
Of waters bruising the white foam of waves
Before whose rush the seagods seek their caves;
Thus, at the music beating through a wall
Tired limbs revive, and shadows seem the tall
And flashing figures walking by a lake;
Known faces, unknown bodies slowly shake
Their dancing skeletons to normal flesh,
And walking in warm light within a mesh
Of memories that follow on the scent
The once again remembered wishes bent
On embraces, or the easier art of flight,
Centre round persons crushed beneath the might
Of phrases blown like trumpets, but to fall
Deafened by loud sound, stifled by the pall
Of soaring wings too heavy for their weight;
The music, dying, ceases, and the mate
Of every big ambition faints away,
Gone are the dreams, the darkness lives, till day
With staring light rehearses all the ills
Poured down on us each morning from the hills.

But now, before ambition starts its reign
And crowns itself within the sleeping brain,

A fitting altar for a mocking rite,
The hours arrive which offer to our sight,
In place of sun motes in a dancing air,
The lively brilliance of crowds laid bare . . .

They glide in carriages past flashing green
Fans, and dropping curtains, liquid with sheen
Of waters, echoing every shaft of light
That fills an avenue too long for sight
Until the gold spoke fits the wheels on high
Moving in majesty along the sky;
From lakes that flash like mirrors or like swords
The echoes send back shuddering sounds and words
And multiply the moving shafts and wells,
Fashion new glory and invent fresh spells
To crack the glass of silence with the tongues
That throw like fountains and have fire for lungs.
They come by water with a white sail, blown
Like a taut cloud, like a gaudy shell shown
Through clear water on the pale plains of sand
As a city with carved towers on gold strand;
Or float more gently, crossing a still world
Using their oars as wings, with wide sails unfurled,
Make the soft sound of feathers as they dip
To wave the water back and press the lip
Floating still further on the troubled glass
That shows its secrets, and the mountain's mass.

A wanton warmness breathes on them below
The shaking smoothness, and white bodies show
That ride the slight waves holding to the manes,
Men on galloping horses down the plains.
Clearer water shows fine limbs that tempt
The dwellers in wild places, rough, unkempt;

If such there were who lived among these woods
Crowding upon the bank, they'd fire their moods
And carry a white body to the caves
To catch the cataracting force of waves,
And gratify the unaccustomed touch;
Soothe with cool snow of limbs the heat, of such
Blind, flowerlike, followers who track the sun
And know the causeways where his feet have run
Treading through clear clouds the treetops, below
He dyes the leaves with brilliance to show
The glittering windows and the shining roofs;
Pavilions that tremble, as his hoofs
Sound in the orchards where he stoops to hang
Gold apples on high trees, through which there rang
Laughter like dropping water, till, sweet tears,
The rain showers fell to dissipate their fears;
Small suffering of short lived pain distil
This elixir of happiness, and still
Among the drums and crystal gongs of rain
Voices are calling and we know the rain
Is ended, and the brilliant fruits begin
To grow to fullness and to paint their skin;
Daring the danger and the treacherous shore,
They swim above the never plundered store
Of shadows, where the finished cup of sky
Contains the waters, and the hills so high,
They touch the trees that wave on the far bank,
And shake the mirrored stillness of their rank.
Green are the safest places in the grass
To hide your comfort from the feet that pass,
And little caves between the trees green dark
Give you their stillness, and no need to hark
For prying voices, while near music rings
To keep the people practising their wings,

For while they tread the tight rope of the tune
And walk on air, through clouds, as if to prune
These flowers which grow in clusters high above
The leaf marked waters, lying there to prove
The strength of silver, or the lure of gold,
As night or day, with cowardly or bold
Appearance bribes with white flowers the waves
Or, with fierce countenance controls his slaves;
Others can rest motionless, apart,
Until the moment for their play can start;
In " caverns," leaf hung bowers," or " grots " they lie,
And live their pastorals before the shy
Pipes or piercing trumpets make this pretence
No longer binding, and no more a fence.

From other windows, other gods may lean:
Their sons mark space with intervals of clean
Waterfalls of ripping light, golden walls;
Protecting proud gods, echo through their halls
New signs and symbols acted in the air,
Unknown to us, but seen by clear eyes there;
And from the windows each can watch his son
Leave Heavens of sparkling brilliance, to shun
The drifting gardens with sweet breathing trees
Blown down the wide sky; for they choose the lees
And sifted dregs of goodness where they find
Sweet fruits of conquest, and of loss, combined.
As soon as ever the deep woods are still,
The hollow valley, and the hanging hill
Murmur with liquid voices, till in turn
The woods reply with fiery sounds that burn
And cleanse the dim night, for the gods to reach
Trees rising like green cliffs above a beach.
The carriages arrive, release their load

Beneath green arches, where the grass is mowed
Smooth as the sea, and through its depth as clear;
The leaves, like men on cliffs, can gaze down sheer
And watch, beneath the dancing boughs of waves,
People leaving carriages like caves,
Step into the sunlight, for a moment blind,
Dazed by the dropping splendour that they find;
They stagger like men in the far flung spray
Of the shivered waves on a stormy day,
But the foam falling like snow down the air
Is dust in wide beams of the sun, whose hair
Gilds the blue zenith that he leaps along
With lionlike limbs and loud voice so strong.

GROUP IV

Actor Rehearsing (from a drawing by Daumier)

> Lo! Thy dread empire chaos! is restored:
> Light dies before thy uncreating word:
> Thy hand, great Anarch! lets the curtain fall,
> And universal darkness buries all.
>   ALEXANDER POPE: *The Dunciad.*

I.

PROLOGUE

A BED, a chair, a table, and a cupboard,
Stand in this bare room and rattle at my tread:
Save for these and a mirror is my room quite bare:
It is empty like a honeycomb that holds no honey
For the sun never comes to load my cell with light.
The paper that strips itself from off the walls
Is canvas dropped away and rotting from its scaffolding:
My moonlight tempered with black smoke—
The magnesium lights that groan before each flare.
It is too dark for reflections to play upon the walls
So I have no gilded lattices against my bruised plaster:
My window panes like broken mirrors
Showing me no starlight, that wood of golden trees—
I'm left with nothing but bare boards and rain soaked ceiling:
The creaking furniture my altar,
And this mirror, broken and misty like my past,
Which I still might look in, could I gather its spent light
Splintered in little pools upon the floor.

The magnesium lights that have no steady flame,
That cannot hover like a star on wings of light,
Poised, with spread feathers that they dip from time to time
In the gold lit water that their passage leaves,
But groan before each flare
Catching their breath because the wind blows strong
Coming at us every way it can
Through cracked windows and between the shafts of scaffolding,
Using what is old and done and what is not yet finished,
Burn less and less;
I wait long moments in the wings until they're ready
As though I stood and waited for their dying words,
Scarce whispered,
And when this puff of strength comes
I walk to the stage front,
Living in this radiance while its lifebeat lasts.
Here am I bathing in this silver water
Speaking with my action while I mouth the words out loud
And move with my metaphors;
Like the salamander while my light lasts
I live in the fire's heart, lit air, or shadowed water;
Just when I've started, when I'm finished like a statue,
Carved and coloured, comprehensible to all,
Living in one moment the whole span of life
Where ten failing years weep no longer than a creaking door
And before the hinge is silent time is mute and sad once more,
The light dies out:
It wheezes and gasps for breath before night stifles it,
Crumbling to white powder that fills and stains the air,

ACTOR REHEARSING

It dies and leaves my eyes dazed,
Smarting with this powder,
While parhelions, those mocking lights, play in the wind—
False mirrors for my acting that my tired eyes project for me.
I make for this starlight and its golden leaves of light,
But they sway too high above my head to help me
And before I can reach to them they flicker and fade out:
I stagger in the darkness turned mute as well as blind,
While the parhelions at some other point of wind,
Fostered by its softness, blow their fires alight once more;
I am left alone in the darkness, stone statue in chill water,
I am left alone in my bare room again,
Hungry and cold.

Here will I stay a little: I'll lie upon my bed
And look for visions, like the painter, on damp plaster,
Making my own images from the mouldering marks of damp:
Or I'll listen to the wind's cheap flute that sets my window dancing—
I'll lie awake and hearken to the barking dogs;
I shall not sleep at all.

Now I have a little light, a fire to warm my hands at,
For the moon like an ember shows above the roofs,
It slants down my ceiling like a patch of snow,
And all else goes dark and dead,
As in winter, when the loaded roofs and trees
Look blacker, shadowed by the white upon them—
I will profit by this warm coverlet of cold,
Narcissus-like I'll look among its beams
Till I find one that answers me:
On hands and knees I crawl across the floor

Feeling with my fingers for a jagged edge to cut me,
When I'll know I've found a fragment of my cracked and broken mirror.
Over by the window I can see a pool of light,
I feel along its edges and I dip my fingers in it,
But they tap like hammers on this ice that shows them clearly
And I hollow with my other hand and lift the pool towards me
For the splintered glass will mirror me if I but catch the light;
I'll look for it waiting for the beams to touch my shoulder:
Slowly they cross the room and come to my side
Lying like a shining cloak to keep me warm,
They flow into the mirror and I see myself—
No harlequin standing at unruffled glass
With motley, ribbed like panes, to catch each prism
So that each different lattice shows another phase of light:
My mirror shows no harlequin,
There is no black mask to bridge my sunken cheeks and hide them,
I have no colours:
I am old, and tired, and worn.
There is no time to sew a suit of colours,
And how could those little flames help my shivering body?
For my cold flesh wants comfort, not the sting of fire.
I am old, and dry, and brittle. I should quickly burn to dust.
If the sun came through this window I should crumble at his touch,
Like the mummy in a cave
When the sun first sees its face again,
Asleep so long;
Like the mummy's are my eyes too, awake and staring,

ACTOR REHEARSING

I am ever looking for the wonders that I said would happen,
But no one ever comes and so I stand alone,
Wondering what will happen.
The glass will just show me my mouth and eyes:
My mouth is an empty purse that will not shut:
My neck when I shift the glass looks gnarled and rigid,
Only strong enough to hold me till my load of air's too heavy:
My hands are a doctor's hands, they divine like clever eyes,
They can see into flesh or bone and find its canker,
Binding bone and muscle that were broken with steel fingers:
I can see above my wrists the jagged cuffs too frayed with wearing,
The patched elbows, and torn pockets
That cannot hold my spectacles
So worn their silken lining:
My coat is frayed and mildewed like a priest's coat green with age.
I tremble ever so little, for my years are like shaking leaves
That rattle before they fall;
I tremble like the starlight through blue leaves of heaven.

I lie here playing like a child with the light,
Imagining, to make me sleep,
That this is not moonlight
Coming through cracked windows in an empty house,
But light poured out
Free and bounteous as light giving trees
That glitter and give shade for all,
This light in golden boughs and shimmering branches
Springing out from windows that are lit and open,
So the space round the house becomes a level shining lawn,

Lucent as a mirror for light to play upon.
Safe in this bounty and hid in these bright beams,
I can sleep beneath a tree and let its golden breath cool me
While the same wind that comforts me plays among the beams,
Mingling light and shadow,
Like the image and its answer out of the mirror's crystal cavern.
If I'm woken by a lull, or pause,
It's worse than never sleeping;
I wake up older by the centuries I've slept
Crushed and broken by one moment's leaded weight.
My life cut off from me by this sharp gulf
Lies beyond where I can touch and lives without me
While I'm powerless to alter it,—
It lies behind me where I cannot reach to it,
As though we were divided by barred windows and the jailor's key,
These waving fields my rain crushed down
Glitter at my window on the gold waves of air
Where my hand could cut and bind the cornsheaves,
While I reaped all day, beating down those bearded regiments,
Binding my prisoners as each batch of them surrendered:
But I never reaped that harvest
For my rain came down and spoilt it,
I soaked it with my own hands and washed its gold away.
My days like that hot summer last still in my memory,
I can go through every moment but I cannot bend its course:
They live like a parallel, a scaffolding built round me
That follows me in everything but never touches me,
So I'm never free to move again,
Or touch that shadow life that lies so near to me.

This shadow, just my own height, is a ghost that follows me.
The staring midday sun, for ever burning, makes it like me,
Aping my own height, while this bitter staring eye
Leaves nothing dark, so my life like one huge plain is lit
And burns from end to end while I am powerless to help it.
All my actions seem pathetic—
The crumpled way I lie to try for sleep,
The book I read before that
Like a hood round the falcon's eyes
That blinds it from the little birds that worry it to follow them,
For the falcon must be fresh and strong to follow its fit quarry;
Everything I have that's near me;
My clothes, worn and dusty, no better for their brushing;
My boots, ragged agents of my footprints on the sands of time,
The cupboard with my best clothes packed in paper;
The table set with pens and ink
To answer if a friend writes to me;
Anything with purpose or possession, makes me sadder;
The things I've done on purpose, little traps to lengthen time
By making life more comfortable;
Or snares to prick time faster by relief of pain;
Possession, any fruit I've picked while passing
Which hunger has not made me eat before I've climbed these stairs
And brought it home to keep;
Anything I've saved out of this wreck on which the waves break,
Rolling in year upon year;
Any hoards I've massed

Joining me with the animals who store up for winter
And hide their treasure bravely in the hostile snow,
Daring fortune;
The tin box with my money; and my evening paper,
That daily programme of disaster
That I read each night, sleeping quieter if the news is bad,
Lulled by calamity;
The thought that this paper had its purpose
To be bought by me,
That there was no other end for it,
That neither of us chose, or had the power to settle,
That had I never paid for it, the paper had no being for me,
For all these things are settled for us
And we are given, as a toy to keep us thinking,
The fancy that we order things, ourselves, to suit our choice.
It is only in our fancy that we pick our way:—
Each will is a drowned man floating in the waves,
Who moves in his own rhythm,
But answers to the wave's huge motion,
Standing, stark and rigid, when the waves break,
And nodding when they gather their green hills again.

Sleep, whose little fence I build each day,
Whose scaffolding bars me from the day before,
Carves out a cave wherein I hide
That screens me from sunlight and the cold flames of night.
This fence that hides those gold heads from me,
That bars me from their bearded fire
Is but lit air,
Clouded and dull again from too much light:
It is a barrier that I have built myself
Walling in an emptiness where I can lie;

A field snared for foxes, with a high wall for wolves;
Where I sleep in grey shadow from the stones the wall is built of:
My rest is forgetfulness, sweet taste of death,
A field that is not hunted, and a cave left dark from day,
Where I am not hungry.

2.

AT HIS MIRROR

"Have I time yet? Has the bell rung?
For I cannot act great Cæsar with my cloak half-hung.
Hold the lantern higher so it lights my head."
The corridors are draughty and as long as a railway,
Icy to tread along, and tiring as a stairway;
Nothing fits; no doors or windows close.

He looks into his mirror and the glass makes him dramatic:
Like the eagle if it answered to the hunter's horn
Screeching through thin air this echo came forlorn:
Like the eagle's voice this echo out of the mirror to his aching self,
For it shows him as he'd have himself before the light,
All else subordinate, the whole world hushed:
Each knoll a cliff, and every tree a brimming cove
Where warriors in blue water wade
As they strike through leaves like the tide upon the sand
And the branches sway and sing like the sighing strand,
While they break out of this green world,
From one mirror to another.
Here shepherds tune their madrigals,
Where rivers, by the sun loosed, run down in waterfalls

Of shaking fleeces, white as wool,
And tune them to their falling, swift and cool
As they ride past those dolphin backs the sunken rocks.

Next he holds himself before this echo
Like a man at a cave's mouth, bold and loud,
Who shouts into its depths and gets his answer back.
Fierce and brazen does he show out of the mirror,
He sees himself in armour, plumed and plated,
Unhelmeted, his thin hair blown back
Like the flag behind its flagstaff in the high,
Shrill wind of his triumph:
He is high up, rolled in glory,
Smooth as water moving in its riverbed
Over hot rocks and treacherous shoals of sand:
There is nothing hostile, no wind to drown his trumpets.
He can choose his personalities and move among them,
Constantly changing,
Like the hare who doubles on his tracks to hide them:
Or keep to one character
Like a dynasty who rules a country,
Playing the same politics whoever guides the play:
He can hold both reins and have the power to choose between them,
Fit into circumstance, or make his own conditions,
Act in his own character, or wear a cloak that's made for him,
For it blows cold in these corridors,
These set scenes built in stone
With porticoes that open like the trumpet's mouth
Carrying his voice along for wind to run with it
Out from these pillars till it hangs upon the air
 Hiding with its brazen wings all other voices quivering there,

That it mutes with these stiff feathers so their tongue cannot be heard:
He drowned all other voices as his plumes shut out the light,
Letting no voice sound and no light shine forth,
For his voice is like wind's breath hushing leaves or water:
The cloak and the trumpet are the weapons that he triumphs with,
The cloak, his character and the trumpet all the words he speaks;
His cloak is at once an ornament and shield,
It hangs round his shoulders with its yellow curls glittering
And hides the stars' gold light
Behind this fleeced and shining palisade.
These fleeced locks, that dangle, turn to waterfalls he cannot hold,
They lie as close together as the trees in a wood
Flashing like the forest that starlight fashioned for him,
Shining at his window,
For its cracked and broken panes made a mirror to their fantasy.
" Too keen this light—that into every corner peers,
But never helps me—
It makes my humour tragic, like water that it shapes to ice,
It hardens my softness, and it brakes my speed.
My breastplate burnished when a strong light shines upon it
Becomes crumpled tin with many dents from wearing;
So much for me as warrior!
I will sing my wheezy madrigals,
As shepherd, into my mirror;
For its depths, with the light behind,
Will make my sparkling water
With the falls that like loud wind sing
In a tumbling sea of boughs;
But my madrigals to those green branches

Reach not,
For they die beneath the leaves
Like my breath upon this mirror
In thin mist dissolving:
And I breathe again, prolonging it,
To see how soon it dies—
I'm playing with my future when I trick this echo,
For quick as it may die,
It's yet more lasting than my speech,
It lives a moment longer in this crystal cavern,
Hold the lantern higher, so it shines upon my hair!
This sun, however hot, will never touch the winter there:
But let the snow lie, deep and clear.
The bell rings, telling me my hour has come."

3.

REHEARSALS

At the Gate

 "Show your papers! The town gates are closed!"
"I will play Hamlet from the ramparts,
The sands of the circus will make me my bleak shore."
 "There is no rust on your armour."
"The hot breath of the corridor will tarnish me."
 "But the ghost?"
"I will raise up a ghost inside your broken mirrors,
Crack me a cloud and that shall be my vapour."
 "Loads of sand, then, and the spent smoke of a cloud:
 What else will you want?"
"Canvas trees for the Chevalier d'Albert,
There must be an avenue for him to ride down:

The leaves make good windows for a cavalier to look
    through:
The shower of gold for Danaë:
Blue sea for Amalthus: for Perimedes
A forge like a fiery cave
At whose tongues he tempers
Those living engines for our passage, all the horses that we
    ride."
  "Any other fictions?"
"The Golden Fleece, if put to it.
In the bay of Colchis where we disembark
There must be boats and a bright light through the trees;
Or Alexis naked, singing to the goats."
  "We will choose among them. You may pass inside."

Rehearsal for Danaë and the Golden Shower

"Moor it fast! I mind not if damp edges spray me.
Where are the winds? I sent them up their ladders—
Answer me, Zephyrs! Can you hear my call?"
  "Aye! Aye! Sir."
"At your posts, then!
And you, hot wind from the South, pay attention!
I shall start off when I hear the horns!"
  "Do I blow at once, Sir?"
"Give me time to speak!
This is a dockyard full of boats a-building
(These clouds all swim like a ship) for my journey:
When I start off, let me find my balance.
My cloud shall sail me, swimming on the tide,
Blown forth with fury from your lionlike mane,
Until, O raging wind from the South,
You wreck me, helpless on the jagged trees,
Too thin, those tossing leaves, for my feet:

Then fall I,
Soaking down like sunlight through the branches
To rattle in a golden rain on Danaë's shuttered window:
She'll waken at my pelting darts
And wait here, wingèd with her raven hair."

Amalthus

Amalthus swimming through the flocks of waves
Held to their fleeces and was dragged along like Ulysses:
He pulled at their wool, and now they swept too fast,
He sank stiff and dead through gelid water
Until crackling amber and the heaped pearls stopped him.
" I drown like Amalthus, and I wake again,
I rise up, weighted with pearls, to the skies' brim.
Lines of rain that hang like shrouds,
Flocks of waves, droves of clouds,
With my load the tides so strong,
Working under the wind will land
Me safe on these shelving plains of sand:
Over that endless meadow I run
Till I come to the cliff's height out of the sun,
There will I hide it deep in a cave
Where flash no trees, but a green wave
Grows up out of the flooded field
To guard this secret that it will not yield."

The Chevalier d'Albert

" Where can I find the Chevalier d'Albert?
For I think that I can bring him just the word he wants."
" If you ride far enough down the avenue
You will see shining roofs like a lake above the trees,
And out from an arch will a cavalier come riding:

Say these words to him—
  ' That which you look for riding all day,
Like a huntsman following his quarry down a wood,
Has not tumbled, do not search the ground.
By the sharp barbs wounded does it wait for you,
Too high, unless you climb up through the branches?
I saw him start up, bough after bough,
But little did he know what lay below him,
For from another branch, like Absalom a-swinging,
There hung another lover by his hair entangled.' "

Alexis

For Alexis,
Blue sea combed by fire,
And sharp berries on the hillside
Where his goats feed.
He is lying in a rock's shade,
Cool as water, singing,
His eyes half-shut with sun.
Those waterfalls,
The bright trees blowing in the wind,
Play high above him:
They will run like crystal rivers
With his song,
Till crags and cloud-hid cliffs can hear him.
He stands up in the rock's shade
And steps into the sun:
Nymphs, if such there be still,
In caves and tree cool grottos
Will leave the shades in which they hide,
And look through the leaves
Upon this shepherd, gold as honey.
But he moves and will not stand still,

He runs as the river flows,
Now he walks upon the wan white sand
To steep his sunlit body in the sea.
Soft and gentle
Are the snowy waves that break there,
They move like the nymphs move
On gentle beds of grass,
For their shepherd, gold as honey,
Lies, floating, in those soft blue fields.

The Golden Fleece

I have set the stage for Colchis,
And the Golden Fleece is not a mile away:
Beach the boats: let them stand on the shore like houses!
Here is the orchard quite sentinelled by light
That watches over the leaves and grass,
Joining their shadows with a web of golden wire.
These quirks and nets, these meshes and these scales,
These are the facets at whose thousand eyes
You wait and stare until you see the light within,
Burning, like the fire of jewels, from the fruit on every branch,
Thus the orchards; but beyond and across the bay,
Where still there are fruit trees like a quiver of little fires,
There shines out clear from the heart of the wood,
As a sunrise cloud wrecked low upon the trees,
The Golden Fleece,
That hangs like a periwig by its heavy curls lifted
From the head of a God as he walked beneath a branch.
The wool is crumbling because no hand has rescued it,
Like a dust of motes it dances in the sunbeams,
Little by little does its beauty die away
Till when you touch it will your hands be stained:

Deep will its glittering blood dye your arms
And all the winds in air come gilded with the flood,
Until you take the fleece and wrap it round your shoulders,
Making it your breastplate and your winter cloak.

Perimedes the Blacksmith

For Perimedes,
A forge, like a fiery cave;
High is the roof to let the centaurs come here.
I will ride in, thumping, like a troop of horse
And hush the madrigals that all the flames sing;
Their voices burn away like ghosts at break of day;
I will ask him in the silence:—
  " Tell me, Perimedes, for you must know,
  Where lives this race that come to you to tend them?
  . . . But if I light again your dying fire,
                    You'll tell me!
  . . . And make it brighter than the sun
                    To light your cave!"
" Well, sir, now that all the woods are cut
No longer can they build their stables in the trees!"
  " Do they speak like men, or neigh like horses?"
" They talk like gurgling streams all night in the valley
And on their way to my forge I hear them singing:
Before you lie down in a field to sleep
Listen with your ear to the ground for their hoof-sound!"
  " And if they're near?"
" Run to them! They'll neigh when they hear you!"

4.

PERFORMANCE

The lights are so low that I cannot see to stumble:
I dare not move, but have to stand,
Stone still,
Like a statue in chill water:

I will go through all my tragedies;
Though no one answers me:
Such is my method: with every character left open
I work by myself, till an echo from steep battlements
Treads down to meet me with iron feet and beaked eagle voice,
Challenging my tragedies.
It is for this I stand here
Speaking in this dark night;
Since starlight—the wood of gold trees at our windows—
That hedge that lies between us—the lit fronds of the footlights—
So dimly burn, and have such chattering warmth
To light us.
This poor heat is our only hope,
This light our only help from heaven,
And that but a travesty,
A sunlight through many mirrors shown.
There is no safety for us,
But what we store ourselves
Against strong tides and fevers:
Put up no more statues, then, but pray for virtue,
For wells of sweet water in this parched, dry sand.
I can show you many characters,

Many moulds to take your metal,
Many voices, pipes and organ notes,
Much music to unravel:
I can strike with the silver key,
But you must tune your notes.

Answer me, answer me, before I drown,
My steely, tragic armour will bear me down:
It is dark, darker still, almost night:
I die in these direful words; I lose my sight:
" Lo; thy dread empire, Chaos! is restored:
Light dies before thy uncreating word:
Thy hand, great Anarch! lets the curtain fall,
And universal darkness buries all."

GROUP V

Fisherman

"Do the fish still glitter in the waterpool?"
"No, sir, they are netted and lie ready for your feasting.
They glittered in the water as a star would shine
If it steered into our vision
And through the day, as in the night,
Swam there to follow:
In point of light more brilliant than the race of stars
Shining in one body where it masks the sun,
The fish in this waterpool glitter like that star in air.
They turn like the star would do and lie there to look at you,
High against this glass wall that lies between,
With staring eyes, dreaming,
Then will stretch and spread their fins,
And in a flash be gone,
Where shadow of the trees, or false sun, mars the water,
Safe hidden in this shade or flame.
Here, then, with limp nets we come to look for them,
And the meshes strain and open wide, once in the water,
Till the fish tap at those windows and now float inside."
"Were they lively when you caught them?"
"They leaped and sprang like horses till we held them fast.
We haul at the nets now and pull them out of water
And the fish come out with them like strong springs of silver,

They frisk and leap to get their breath like young horses
Galloping through the fields at early morning,
When the sun is strong already,
And the wind whips, like green rye, the running grassland.
Hold the net tightly as it comes to land,
Sagging, while water lines the strings and drops in runlets,
Safe upon the grass now while the fish still leap!
Close bound within the meshes so they cannot move,
Their lightning fettered, they are lifted shoulder-high
To drown there, stifling in the stiff, cold air."

Wind as Husbandman

Wind is husbandman, the sun's heat carrying,
He fills fruit with ripeness and he loads the vines,
More gentle than sunlight, bringing rain to cool them,
For like our tender eyes that cannot look upon the sun,
Fruit and harvest die without the shade, their nurse—
Wind most surely is the sun's ally,
Who works with him, running where his word commands,
Who fetches him his goatskins filled with rain
At his want to loose their necks and let the rain outpour,
While upon his back each slackening skin he carries
And empties them, now here, now there, with uncertain hand.

At the cockcrow sound of trumpets,
Feather crested, when the sun first shows,
Comes wind, hot footed, to make ready the arena
And drives forth the clouds who graze so low upon the plain,
Like a flock the giants among them, while the little clouds

Rest, till he moves them with their sails close set
Like ships that lie the night through for the wind to blow,
Their canvas ready and the sailors on the look-out
Though the same stars burn there and are answered in the water,
Each fire heart blazing low, and never lifted on a wave,
Like fruit to blow there,
Till a wavecrest, for the leaves, now hides it.
Foam shows, and the waves are leaping
Each time they scatter hiding down this image
While, in the sky, the stars burn with fainter fire.

It is wind who into morning air, silent, creeps
And breathes upon its windows with thin mist to hush the stars,
Blowing out those candles, for the young day is born,
And as light burns fiercer, grows the wind more strong
Filling out their sails now so the clouds can start,
And they tack straight down the heavens with the seawind helping.
But he plays with other measures on the high hills walking
For against them, as horizon, he will heap the clouds
Piling white hill on hill to mock their snow,
And the sun, when he comes climbing, for a moment shows,
First his fiery crest, and then his plumes too bright to look at:
Next, to teach the mountains of his fearful might,
The sun, with hot shadow of his flame, attacks the clouds,
But his echo is a fiercer bolt than any lightning,
And, while he looks at them, the clouds are crumbled,
Drifting in split fragments from the mountain mass:
They scatter on the wind like little drifts of snow,
And the sun in his zenith burns without a shade.

Wind, in these summer days, works for the reaper,
Both of them stooping in the golden corn
And while the reaper bows down, stiff with his labour,
Wind plays about his ears and shakes the grain:
In those fields more burnished where the bee works,
There will wind shake and cause to tremble
That glittering harvest, till the bee with his garnering
Leaves the shaking golden bell, and spreads his wings.

GROUP VI

From *Canons of Giant Art: Twenty Torsos in Heroic Landscapes*

Fugal Siege

(In the manner of Mantegna, inspired by his predelle from the altar-piece of San Zeno in the museum at Tours)

REX Tremendæ Majestatis
The start of every rhythm from its nothing burned;
This was the Dawn, the steepfoot redhot Day,
From the straw of the heavens, from the shovelled clouds,
It lit, like fire from tinder, and first reached the grapes
Before it came down lower to the hero's eyes,
For there were warriors, then, and dark blood in the vines.

This was a symbol: in the honey hive
A snub nosed sentry drummed upon the rafter,
And woke her sisters for the harvesting,
Who left the convent lattice in their gold flecked velvet
And dawdled no more but spread their wings and went,
They shone, for that moment, as the sun motes in a beam
And then the pillar lifted and its glitter left it.
The rabbit at the arch of his own labyrinth appeared
And looked, and knew it safe, and let his young come out
To play in piebald light that ever strengthened and grew steeper,
Below the dappled plane tree, stained and marked as if with milk.

This was on earth, and in the higher air
The fires of sunbirth fell upon the mountains
Till they were coals in all that reddest flame,
Embers, bones, or rocky skeletons,
That looked hot to touch in that hollow, hard light;
As phantoms, spectres, were the hills in shadow,
That the sun saw not yet, for they were still in Night.
Hard polished brilliance of the leaves and pebbles,
Close to each other, all alive and separate,
Dwelling apart, as in a world their own,
Struck at the eyes but called no louder than each other,
All having equal claims; the poplar bough
Held its rattles still, its disk-like leaves,
While the stones shone as jewels from the glass clear stream
And a fly walked the timber of the wooden bridge;
There was nothing hidden, there was no escape,
This was Day reviewing all its hordes
And not a leaf, not a pebble, must be out of place;
The mountains were as walls, or towers, celestial bastions,
Till, Mantegna-like, a cloud came down
And lay, quite still, along their battlements;
It rode, a ship at anchor, by the safety of those cliffs,
And the prow of this galley, like a goddess carved,
Had long flowing body, flowing hair, deep lidded eyes,
All growing of the cloud's untrammelled snow.
The grapes had their blueness and their rich soft bloom,
Velvet as the bee's lips and more honeyed,
Since sweetness broke from them as dew in summer,
And the sun on the shining grapes was all the warrior's Dawn
As they woke and saw that mystery in the clouds
Drop her virginity and drift in smoke:
By now, the great azure in its might and fire,
Flamed absolute, and reigned in all the ether,

The deeper dire tremendous splendour
Opened the firmament unto its ends
And showed the emptiness, though none dared look.

Though this was day, not all the world had slept
For the siege and its ardours were awake for ever
Pacing the ramparts by loud light of torches
While every footfall was a moment, or an hour,
A day on the seashore listening to the waves
As if this was Elsinore and the empty Sound,
With not a sail, and nothing but the bleached bare cliffs:
But that was the North, the hollow land of ghosts,
Here, the first moving thing the eyes could see
Was a tortoise crawling in the painful grass,
While the stork and the ibis veered above
Looking for their nests as if they'd lost them,
Though they showed as big as turbans on the ruined walls:
Thus did they stretch themselves and throw off sleep,
In the clear hyaline, the diamond morning,
Floating, level winged, through all the pride of air;
And, below, the heroes of the siege were stirring:
Their plumèd helmets—were the warriors buried standing?
Stood lifeless, empty, at the tent mouth;
But this was no funeral, no long lament,
For presently the clarion blew with shivering brass
And before that tumult died the glitter of bright armour
Told that the day's battles had begun again.

The spectres and their masters moved, and they were horse and man,
On the hot, naked shore among the waves' white flanges
Deep in some pompous mystery, some settled purpose,
While they flickered like a statue's shadow caught between
    two worlds,

Belonging neither to the sea nor earth,
For they moved on knife edges of the light's sharp lines
Where sea and the salt shore, stained and pale,
Divided, fought for them;
But the secret voices of the wind came near
For this parade of spectres grew taller and yet taller,
Their horses' heads were turned, they came back slow
Making a hundred statues at those borders of two worlds,
Sometimes a victory, a pose of plume and mane,
Or a statue conquering the sea,
For the stallions curvetted and trod more air than sand;
This was a pantomime, a play of their machinery,
And they tried all possibility, all poses of their bodies,
Trying their white statuary on the salt pale shore.
The sea had all the colour, and the dun, bare land
Nor rocks, nor cactuses,
No sharp points pricking at such easy harmony,
So the men and horses were alone upon the earth
In a stone solitude their statues filled.

This was the only silence, for stern heroic voices
Spoke their magic syllables as spirits in the air,
These were the ancestral shades at their prophecy of war
Who uttered at deep intervals, foretelling doom,
Their words came from nowhere, out of hidden lips,
It might have been the rocks, or the hollow hills, that spoke
For there was never warning till the clear words came
In frightful menace, shuddering the flesh;
Priam and Paris, all the heroes of the siege,
With Cassandra and Hecuba, Hector and Achilles,
These were names that were as lead upon the air,
Falling, clattering, breaking, on the stony ground,
They were winning or losing, they were battle labels
To give the siege its phases, to divide its ardours,

But death, and only one death, was for all
For all were mortal and could not go among the gods
To sleep in fields of poppies and come back refreshed again
For another life in armour to the trumpet drilled,
Obeying those clanging words, those eagle lips,
In cruel injunction and mysterious restraint
That make the hazards of a hero's task,
By starving and sharpening his natural wants.

Such lives are a desert with no honey in it
Where arms and armour were the only bright thing,
But with this much in it, that immortal life
Could have no bettering, no prize to win,
And here, this prison, this steel upon the chest,
Grew light and was lifted at each hazard won;
Wind blew a breath of flowers more drowsy than those poppies,
And lulled each sleeping head with dreams of more,
Granting perpetuity, a stay of time,
Another opportunity when dead days burned once more
And the same things, like a clock, came past,
All altered by little moves to what they might have been.

Here Heaven suffered by its certainties,
Where nothing could lapse and all the fates were fixed,
Falling through Time as if with stones tied to their feet:
And this made immortality another prison
And one more desperate for thicker walls
That nothing could break, that had no bars to snap,
And this was spaceless, fathomless, in blinding light,
Painful from its glare, impenetrable, dreadful,
Aching in an ecstasy just ended, drooping;
For this was endless living with no death to come,
No dreads, nor fears, nor any late fulfilment;

Not thus did the siege last but in a smaller world
Spiced with uncertainty, with chance and hazard,
Where all things might happen, where the dead's dire voices
Warned to no purpose; they were empty threats
Urging both sides as if both sides obeyed,
Two voices out of one hell shrieked advice
And there was nothing but this hell beyond,
No other alternative, no place but death.

But this is Dawn, when death is near and kind,
He snares the dying man with sleep and no more pain
While sweet breath morning fills the fœtid room;
Pay no more heed to them, the dying and the dead,
Hark, hark to the trumpets out of the draughty, bitter barracoon
Calling the hours, the falling hand of Time,
That drops by degrees, that is steady and relentless;
At its word the great engines of the siege are strummed,
And all their plucked and rattling strings, released,
Pelt their great hailstones out of heaven on the walls,
Rattling, echoing, and rebounding, rolling.
Stay! Be not frightened! There's no more than this,
It's the draughty, bitter barracoon, the fort or tower,
With a ghost or two in armour to defend the walls:
What will it matter if their steel is dented?

The siege is but a bruise upon the flower thick hills,
A trampling of the clover as if a crowd had been there;
Even in the vines the shouts and clamour die,
There's nothing the matter, there's no right or wrong,
The grape's blue bunches like a shower in the hand
Have all the summer's sweetness to themselves alone,
Should there be more than this the flowers are here
Who will breathe their savour, soft as dew upon the lips;

FUGAL SIEGE

Bow down your head and touch the petals with your mouth
For it is like sleep and now the siege is hidden;
Who could know, lying in this lily field,
Of that unhappy horror, age old cancer,
Eating the summer and its painted flowers?
Those longer days that only gave more light
They made their blessing that the summer yielded them,
Burning that plenty with a sharp, quick flame,
Made fiercer from waiting, from the hunger for it;
There's something more than this, some palliation,
Hark the blaring tumult of the trumpet!

The pompous marching in the labyrinth,
By fallen arches, statues toppled down,
Lying, dead warriors in the circus dust,
As if their fall had pleased a theatre crowd:
This labyrinth, a maze of empty ruins,
All echoing, answering the trumpet call;
These are the meadows where that music broods,
It likes the ruins for the noise they give,
As rumbling caves, or shells held to the ear,
For the sound comes back to them and dies not at the lips;
They hold its continuance, the surfeit of its life,
As their own image, held before their eyes,
Which moves when they move, copies them in all,
So that it is their surety, their proof of life;
Why wonder at its mysteries which are so clear,
At pride and arrogance, the puffing out of emptiness?
Enter, instead, into that inner, empty heart
And know its neediness, its fireless altar,
When all the cold airs gathered there
Cry for their freedom from that sealed up tomb
And burst the walls and run from them,
Shivering as a dying cry on lips that Death has parched,

That are sore and broken, that dread what is to come to them.
So the peals of triumph are despair broke loose,
The trumpet and the rolling drum
Mean no more than this and have no other secret,
Desire and regret have made that ten years' siege,
Which two dire forces are parents of all poetry:
The siege and its ardours are alive for ever,
As never dying poetry, as music echoing,
Such are their marches in gardens by the water side,
The Babylonian splendour, striking terror like a massacre,
The snarling trumpet's pride, the thunderstorm of war drums,
These are their parables, the scaffolds of their buildings,
That never can have life, they are but thrown into the air
To hang there for a breath and fall again in ruin,
Dropping from the other towers, the permanent, the standing ones,
That nothing can destroy, so all the siege is vain;
Vain, but not profitless, for see its spoils,
Which ever have been, and will be for eternity,
For this was how poetry and music came:
They formed at the lips and got no further than the air,
Having no flesh, but only breath to fill them.

Pastoral

(*From the two golden cups of Vaphio in the Museum at Athens*)

BEGIN with water:
All is rock and water:
Drink from the waterfall, that once was snow,
In its sleep, its chrysalis;

That, now, has wings,
That flashes, leaps, and tumbles,
That is living water;
This cavern, this poplar grove, this briar of berries,
Bread, oracle and altar,
And the living water;
A hive of honey and a stook of corn,
This is my beginning, this the oaten air,
The song of barley, the whisper of the wheat,
The shepherd's music, the sunbright heat.

It strengthens, it thickens, it is breath, itself;
Come, walk by the cornfield, and listen! Listen!
Where else, but of ocean, is there so much sound,
A sighing, a rustling, not a noise of sea,
But a secrecy, a whispering, a lulling of the oats;
And wind blows the smoke, it is the world of men
And air hammers, hammers, all the earth is theirs.

Air hammers, hammers, it is dawn of day,
They are cutting firewood, they have fed the flames
With limbs of cypress, to the sound of bronze
Hewn, hewn with hatchets, till the dyed, stained air
Reeks with cypress smoke; and in this early age
Smoke means men are near, their might is fire,
Fire is their divinity, they worship fire;
They live in simplicity, in no count of time,
Leading their flocks along the aromatic hills
In sight of the sea and its unnumbered isles
Where wonder dwelt, before the rising of the sun,
In the land of the river, where the tents of stone
Pyramids, triangles, forever pitched,
Held the first Pharaohs, and may hold them still.

This is Hellas with no orators, before the Hellenes,
Hellas of no statues, and of unhewn marble
Still in the quarry, in the mountain's womb,
Unborn, not dreaming yet, not taking shape;
They speak another language, a forgotten tongue
Untuned to these waters, to this limestone land;
It runs not in poetry, too rough its chime
For the lifting seaweed, the nearly noiseless tide
That nods, night and day, nods and wakens in the rocks;
Nor runs with the corn; nor is the air on cliffs;
Nor lights on armour, nor low notes of the lute;
Homer is unborn, and all of Troy unburnt.

But all their history is the island of Mount Ida,
Of labyrinth and minotaur, of the white bull and the virgins;
Their men are men of Knossos, they are bitter fanged,
Drawn out of canon as shadows of the slope
On steepfoot mountain in the slanting sun,
Tall and thin as that, of waspish waists
By belts of bronze, slipped to their middle when they scarce
    could walk,
Imprisoned, never growing; by their milky fare
Eased to this stricture, who only ate of meat
At bloodshed offering from the altar of the fire,
Heaped with cypress, and now marked by blood;
Their women, as those women, as the priestesses,
For days of such sacrifice, in ghosts of the serpent,
In snake-like puffings, in a skirt of hoops,
Bare bosomed, necklaced, with wide-ribbed sleeves,
Dressed as the goddess, and for stature coiffed
With a high diadem, a mitred headdress;
Bare armed for the snake to crawl, to hold the serpent
In flickering lightning that darted from their fingers.
Life could not be all pastoral, so near the sea,

PASTORAL

With half the world of water, with all straightness barred
And the near hill an island in profoundest main,
Depthless, of deep shadows of the clouds upon it;
They netted the dark water, and it sparked with fire,
It shone, it gleamed, it glittered, it had scales of silver,
It was a shining dagger, hurled and quivering
That flashed in the meshes; now the whole net moved,
The fish leaped and flapped in it, with nervous fin
Springing for the water, to be lost once more,
Missed, slipped, fell again, were drowned in air,
And, dying, prinked their colours to more glorious and violent;
Cerulean, incredible, of unreal blue,
In gold drops speckled, in a gold splashed rain,
Of snow on lapis, or of leopard spots,
Burning in the blueness, so parhelion bright,
They were little mimic suns, or drops of boiling oil
Too soon consumed and dying with the breath.
The fins were rays of gold, spread wings of fire
Too fine for plumes, but more like lateened sails
To move them through the waters, and for oar and rudder
To steer them to the great deeps, or up into the light
Where salt sweet tresses of the seaweed moved
In maiden softness and with maiden sighs,
Sadly, sadly, in the lapping tides

. . . . . .

In delight of the sea pools, so their pastoral life
Lay in two worlds, they were fisherman and shepherd.

Warrior hearted, with no one to fight,
They go out, at morning, and we meet them in the groves
Moving down the shadow, as in mimic war,
In wait on the wind, to attend upon its changes,
Halting at a lull, creeping forward at its blowing,

At back of the herd, and with wind against them
In full morning of the waisthigh plain,
Working to the battlefield, a burnt up space
With floor of fine stubble that the feet can hold,
Here, by show of slavery, to make more slaves,
Let tamed lead untamed to decoy of doom.

These are no shepherds of Sicilian shade,
Ephebus of river bank, in beauty bathing
Honey brown, nubile, near flagellant reeds,
Strato's darling, pretty Corydon,
But men of the helmet, of the metal waist,
Ripe for the bull, and of no other weapon,
No spear, no shield, and but a coil of rope;
As fight of wasp and beetle, as thin wire to armour,
Their pride, their thinness, when the wild bulls come,
And see the milchkine and would go among them,
Lowing, mild and gentle, while they make their choice,
But stop, sniff the air, and turn their dreadful heads
At man, first men they knew, as though forewarned,
Forewarned and furious, to fearful loudness,
Of leather, of brass, of every roaring wind,
In bull throat mightiness wording forth their strength
In shaking, long thunder, to the earth confused;
And stand, stockstill; and then the blast is loosed
Of speed, mass, movement, in mighty charge
Of blind, brute force, not seeing and not hearing.

This is wasp and beetle, wiry sinew against armour,
For man fights bull, he is no bigger than its thigh,
In no armour of hide, nor pair of pointed horns;
This is his epic, the taming of the bull,
We see him on the treasure cups, the golden bowls,
Made immortal, left forever in the tomb;

Man's subtlety to man was not subtlety to force,
This was more glorious, it was man and earth,
Most giant strength, mightiest brute of all,
Whom we would not kill, but would mate him to his cattle.

The gold cups show this, how the stratagem
Worked in the meadow, by the sycamore;
There were but few men to all the herd of kine
And they moved, unafraid, to where a ropen net
Swung from two trees and diapered the shadow,
Here two men hid, while others came behind,
And the great armada, vast, leviathan,
Of wild bulls followed them, at peace with all,
The King bull in this harem, in that new found plenty,
Content and incurious, in the lozenged shade.

The iron men drink; it is a feast of wasps,
For they come in striped fleeces through the rasp of smoke
And like a wasp figure to its sheath of wings
So are their metal waists below the wool,
As they sit by the fire to lift the golden bowls;
It is drinking from a mirror, for their deeds are carved,
Their hands of that history have held the cups
In the autumn moonlight, in the hunter's moon,
Have drunk above the sycamore, have pressed their lips
To the heartbeat air around the pointed horns,
Have dwelt in that danger, and have drunk again
And are dust, only dust, and yet the day lives on.

O look at the hunter's moon, the autumn lantern,
It is golden as ripe barley, as the yellow bowls,
As the light of cornsheaves held against the brim,
Nodding, nodding, nodding, in a noon of sleep!
O wake not the sleepers, lest they go to dust,

But leave them in the moonlight, it is some sort of life,
Better than death, to live upon these bowls,
At the feast, after the hunting, when all men are tired.
Come, drink again, come haunt it with your lips,
So we see your strange shadows by the fishing nets,
Be shepherd, be fisherman, go look for bulls;
The shepherds who come after you will idle in the shade,
We want no idylls, or would listen to the leaves,
This shall be morning, that is afternoon,
The slant of the sun; we want the whitehot morning.
This is no Sicily, no ghost of snow,
No cloud of cold Etna cools a molten sea;
This is rock and water; it is the hour of wasps,
They fang the ripe fruit; and we have men, as these,
Who eat the cuttle fish, who hunt the bull,
Heroes shall spring from them, foreshadowing whom,
These cups are haunted, they are sacred vessels.
O look once more at them, the iron men move
As the lights of sky, from rim to rim of it;
They fight the earth, they capture it, they tame the bulls;
This is their mirror where they pledged themselves,
Their lips touched the brim above the golden image;
These cups were held by demi-gods, by the first men,
By demi-gods, not shepherds, in a hunter's moon,
Like the light of corn sheaves held against the bowls.
O wake not the sleepers! Let them sleep! sleep on!

Agamemnon's Tomb
   (At Mycenæ)

TOMB
   A hollow hateful word
A bell, a leaden bell the dry lips mock,
Though the word is as mud or clay in its own sound;
A hollow noise that echoes its own emptiness,
Such is the awful thing, this cell to hold the box.
It is breathless, a sink of damp and mould, that's all,
Where bones make dust and move not otherwise;
Who loves the spider or the worm, for this,
That they starve in there, but are its liveliness?
The gravecloth, coldest and last nightgown,
That's worn forever till its rags are gone,
This comes at the end when every limb is straight,
When mouth and eyes are shut in mockery of sleep.
Much comes before this, for the miser hand
That clutches at an edge of wood, a chair, a table,
Must have its fingers broken, have its bones cracked back,
It's the rigor mortis, death struggle out of life,
A wrestling at the world's edge for which way to go.

There are all other deaths, but all are sisters;
What dreams must they have who die so quiet in sleep,
What dread pursuings into arms of terror,
Feared all through life, gigantic in dark corridors,
A giant in a wood, or a swirling of deep waters;
This may be worst of all, for pain is material,
And it has its lulls, or you may pray for them,
While, when the pain is worst, you pray for death,

For swift delivery from heart and lungs,
The tyrant machinery, the creaking engine,
Lungs like wheezing bellows, heart like a clock that stops;
To die frightened, with a scream that never comes,
That shivers with no shape out of the dumb dry lips,
This is worse than pain, and worse than death, awake,
For with that cry you're in the tomb already,
There's its arch above you, there's its hand upon your mouth.
Knock, knock, knock, these are the nails of the coffin,
They go in easy, but must be wrenched out,
For no strength can break them from the walled night within;
They are little shining points, they are cloves that have no scent,
But the dead are kept in prison by such little things,
Though little does it help them when that guard is gone.
It is night, endless night, with not a chink of day,
And if the coffin breaks there is no hope in that,
The bones tumble out and only dogs will steal them;
There is no escape, no tunnel back to life,
And, soon, no person digging at the other end,
For the living soon forget, but soon will join you there;
The dead are but dead, there is no use for them,
But who can realize that it ends with breath,
That the heart is not a clock and will not wind once more!
There is something in mortality that will not touch on death,
That keeps the mind from it, that hides the coffin;
And, if this were not so, there would be nought else,
No other thing to think of; the skull would be the altar,
There could be no prayer save rest for the skeleton
That has jagged bones and cannot lie at comfort;

AGAMEMNON'S TOMB

The sweetest flowers soon wither there, they love it not.
Who pondered too much on this would lie among the bones
And sleep and wake by little contrast there,
Finding them no different but always cold;
The hermit's only plaything was the death's head in his cell,
That he was long used to, that never stared at night
Through eyes without lids, kissed away by something,
With a mouth below that, bare and lipless,
Eaten by the dust, quite burned away;
But the hermit was not frightened, he had grown accustomed,
For it is one sort of logic to be living with the dead,
It's so slight a difference, a stone dropped from the hand
Picked up not long ago, now dropped again;
This is one remedy, to know the dead from near,
But it ends at nothing, there's no more than that,
The fright of death goes, but not the dreading of its dullness;
It is endless, dull, and comfortless, it never stops,
There is no term to it, no first nor last,
There is no mercy in that dark land of death.
Think of death's companions, the owl, the bat, the spider,
And they can only enter when the tomb is broken,
They live in that darkness, in that lair of treachery,
And crawl, and spin their webs, and shake their speckled wings,
And come out in the double night, the night that's dark outside
So they bring no light back on their fattened bodies.
The spider, with its eight legs, runs and crawls,
With dreadful stomach, hairy paunch in air,
While the bat hangs, asleep, with gripping claws above
Holding to the stone ledge fouled by it;
He'll wake, when it's night outside, and wave his skinny wings,

And fly out through the crevice where the spider weaves anew,
Her silk will choke and fill it when the bat comes back,
And the bat, more clumsy, rends the webs asunder.
Such are death's companions and their twilit lives,
They keep by dry bones and yet they profit by them,
Living on death's bounties, on his dying portion,
Paid like marriage money, or the fees for school;
This, in stone or marble, is the home of others,
For they share it, but too soon, and it is theirs no more.
There is nothing at the other end, no door at which to listen,
There is nothing, nothing, not a breath beyond,
Give up your hopes of it, you'll wake no more.

The poor are fast forgotten,
They outnumber the living, but where are all their bones?
For every man alive there are a million dead,
Has their dust gone into earth that it is never seen?
There should be no air to breathe, with it so thick,
No space for wind to blow, nor rain to fall;
Earth should be a cloud of dust, a soil of bones,
With no room, even, for our skeletons;
It is wasted time to think of it, to count its grains,
When all are alike and there's no difference in them;
They wait in the dark corridors, in earth's black galleries,
But the doors never open; they are dead, dead, dead.
Ah! Seek not the difference in king or beggar:
The King has his gold with him, that will not buy,
It is better to have starved and to be used to it.
Is there no comfort down the long dead years,
No warmth in prison, no love left for dead bones;
Does no one come to kiss them? Answer, none, none, none.

AGAMEMNON'S TOMB

Yet that was their longing, to be held and given,
To be handed to death while held in arms that loved them,
For his greater care, who saw that they were loved
And would take note of it and favour them in prison;
But, instead, he stood more near to them, his chill was in them,
And the living were warm, the last of love was warm;
Oh! One more ray of it, one beam before the winter,
Before they were unborn, beyond the blind, unborn,
More blind and puny, carried back into the dark,
But without rumour, with no fate to come,
Nothing but waiting, waiting long for nothing.

It was too late to weep, this was the last of time,
The light flickered, but tears would dim it more:
It was better to be calm and keep the taste of life;
But a sip or two of life, and then, forever, death.
Oh! The cold, the sinking cold, the falling from the edge
Where love was no help and could not hold one back,
Falling, falling, falling into blackest dark,
Falling while hands touched one, while the lips felt warm,
If one was loved, and was not left alone.

Now it was so little that a babe was more,
No more of self, a little feeble thing
That love could not help,
That none could love for what it was;
It looked, and love saw it, but it could not answer:
Life's mystery was finished, only death was clear,
It was sorry for the living, it was glad to die,
Death was its master, it belonged to death.

O kiss it no more, it is so cold and pale,
It is not this world, it is no part of us;

Not the soul we loved, but something pitiful
The hands should not touch. Oh! Leave it where it lies;
Let the dead where they die; come out among the living;
Weep not over dead bones; your tears are wasted.
There's no escape, there is no subterfuge,
Death is decay; nor was it any better,
The mummied dead body, with brain pulled through the nose,
With entrails cut out, and all the mutilation
Wrapped in sweet bandages, bound up with herbs:
Death is not aromatic, it is false with flowers,
It has no ferment, it is always bitter;
The Egyptians live for ever, but not like themselves,
They are clenched, tortured, stifled, not the portrait on the lid;
They'd be better as old bones, and then might lie at peace.

All is degradation in the chambers of dead bones,
Nor marble, nor porphyry, but make it worse
For the mind sees, inside it, to the stained wet shroud
Where all else is dry, and only that is fluid,
So are carven tombs in the core to their cool marble,
The hollowed out heart of it, the inner cell,
All is degradation in the halls of the dead;
I never thought other things of death, until
The climb to Mycenæ, when the wind and rain
Stormed at the tombs, when the rocks were as clouds
Struck still in the hurricane, driven to the hillside,
And rain poured in torrents, all the air was water.
The wet grey Argolide wept below,
The winds wailed and tore their hair,
The plain of Argos mourned and was in mist,
In mist tossed and shaken, in a sea of wrack;
This was the place of weeping, the day of tears.

AGAMEMNON'S TOMB

As if all the dead were here, in all their pain,
Not stilled, nor assuaged, but aching to the bone;
It was their hell, they had no other hope than this,
But not alone, it was not nothingness:
The wind shrieked, the rain poured, the steep wet stones
Were a cliff in a whirlwind, by a raging sea,
Hidden by the rainstorm pelting down from heaven
To that hollow valley loud with melancholy;
But the dark hill opened. And it was the tomb.

A passage led into it, cut through the hill,
Echoing, rebounding with the million ringing rain,
With walls, ever higher, till the giant lintel
Of huge stone, jagged and immense, rough hewn
That held up the mountain: it was night within:
Silence and peace, nor sound of wind nor rain,
But a huge dome, glowing with the day from out
Let in by the narrow door, diffused by that,
More like some cavern under ocean's lips,
Fine and incredible, diminished in its stones,
For the hand of man had fitted them, of dwindling size,
Row after row, round all the hollow dome,
As scales of fish, as of the ocean's fins,
Pinned with bronze flowers that were, now, all fallen,
But the stones kept their symmetry, their separate shape
To the dome's high cupola of giant stone:
All was high and solemn in the cavern tomb:
If this was death, then death was poetry,
First architecture of the man made years,
This was peace for the accursed Atridæ:
Here lay Agamemnon in a cell beyond,
A little room of death, behind the solemn dome
Not burnt, nor coffined, but laid upon the soil
With a golden mask upon his dead man's face

For a little realm of light within that shadowed room:
And ever the sun came, every day of life,
Though less than starpoint in that starry sky,
To the shadowed meridian, and sloped again,
Nor lit his armour, nor the mask upon his face,
For they burned in eternal night, they smouldered in it;
Season followed season, there was summer in the tomb,
Through hidden crevice, down that point of light,
Summer of loud wings and of the ghosts of blossom;
One by one, as harvesters, all heavy laden,
The bees sought their corridor into the dome
With honey of the asphodel, the flower of death,
Or thyme, rain sodden, and more sweet for that;
Here was their honeycomb, high in the roof,
I heard sweet summer from their drumming wings,
Though it wept and rained and was the time of tears;
They made low music, they murmured in the tomb,
As droning nuns through all the shuttered noon,
Who prayed in this place of death, and knew it not.

How sweet such death, with honey from the flowers,
A little air, a little light, and drone of wings,
To long monotony, to prison of the tomb!
But he did not know it. His bones, picked clean,
Were any other bones. The trick is in our mind:
They love not a bed, nor raiment for their bones,
They are happy on cold stone or in the aching water,
And neither care, nor care not, they are only dead.
It once was Agamemnon, and we think him happy:
O false, false hope! How empty his happiness,
All for a fine cavern and the hum of bees.

I went again to him, another year,
And still it stormed, the corn ripe Argolide

AGAMEMNON'S TOMB

Rattled in dust, in burning grain of sand,
Earth lay in fever by the tombed Atridæ.
O happy, happy death, and only happiness of that,
There is none other, where it ever weeps
In the ripened corn and round the silent cavern,
First, and best building of the man made years!
O happy Agamemnon, who was luckless, living,
Happy in death, in the hollow haunted room,
Your very name is the treading of a spectre:
O speak to us of death, tell us of its mysteries,
Not here, not here, not in the hollow tomb,
But at the Muse's fountain, the Castalian spring,
By the plane trees you planted, in the sacred shade;
The leaves speak in syllables, the livelong hours,
Their leaves are your leaves, and their shade is yours;
Listen, listen, listen to the voice of water
Alive and living, more than Agamemnon,
Whose name is sound of footsteps on the shaking boards,
A tragedian's ghost, a shadow on the rocks.
You are dead, you are dead, and all the dead are nothing to us,
There's nothing, nothing, nothing, not a breath beyond:
O give up every hope of it, we'll wake no more,
We are the world and it will end with us:
The heart is not a clock, it will not wind again,
The dead are but dead, there is no use for them,
They neither care, nor care not, they are only dead.

From *Battles of the Centaurs*
(Centaurs and Lapithæ)

WHITE clouds
(White stallions, white horses tethered),
Make tents and sails and side walls for the banquet:
The trestles are laid: Hippodamia is feasted.

She was born in Argos, where masks of gold
Hide the dead faces in the dead men's tombs:
In beauty as the Argolide, the golden land,
For her skin is saffron, or is smoky amber
Smouldering to the sullen mouth, the red, red lips,
Disdainful, cruel, as a cup of poison
To taint the eyes and kill the souls of men
Caught in the fronds of her, her saffron locks.

She marries Pirithous, King of the Lapithæ:
The gods are invited, all the gods but Mars:
And the Heroes of the days of gold:
And the Centaurs, their neighbours:
The banquet opens.

Round her lie the gods,
And Heroes, Giants and Warriors, who feast their loves,
All happy for an hour, for an immortal breath:
The Centaurs as an army on the grass,
Lie down for the feast, and are men above the trestles
Lifting the wine bowl
To a tune of conches:
Pirithous, beside her, never looks at else
But dwells on her lips, or is lost among her curls.

BATTLES OF THE CENTAURS

More wine, more wine, and music while we drink,
Of lute and reed, but not the martial drum;
Let the lute be our hearts on fire that tremble in the heat,
Let the reed be the cooling voice, the agony of the flame;
Music, more music, let us live on fire!

But Mars puts his minions to the kettledrums;
The leaden thunder triumphs;
With his burning blood
Eurythion, a Centaur, leans to Hippodamia,
Pulls her saffron curls to him, with wine stained fingers,
And presses his lips to hers, not unreluctant.
He holds her head above him, as a cup to drink,
And drinks from her lips, and holds her saffron fronds
Looking on her amber skin, her sullen smooth amber,
As parchment with flame behind, as smoke on amber,
And drinks his immortality, his fill of her,
Kissing till the breath goes.

Pirithous sees them, and the Heroes fly to arms,
Hercules, Theseus, the Lapithæ all;
Mars won his stratagem and started war,
Wine stains the trestles, Hippodamia's eyes
Watch her lover go from life to death,
Struck down at her lips;
The breath of her fails in him, he faints and dies
While the dagger shakes,
And Hippodamia, all saffron and all honey,
Smiles for Pirithous with the same red lips.

Eurythion fell, and his body of a Centaur
Sagged, sagged, crumpled,
As though fallen from a cliff;
Other Centaurs dashed their wine bowls down,

The metal battle started, loud the din of armour,
Dented from thrown cups, from emptied bottles hurled
To the breasts of bronze.
The Centaurs held the day until the Heroes found their arms,
And only Eurythion, who drank death from her lips,
Walks in darkness, in the outer world
Waiting for a shadow, another Centaur on the sands,
Or Hippodamia, as he dreamed of her,
Fled from men to meet him,
In her saffron fronds.

The Lapithæ rally, and the Heroes of high names,
In armour of bronze, with horsetail helm
Blown straight with speed, as in the gallop's thunder;
Hercules is with them, in Nemæan coat
Of tawny lion, slain at the Argive wood
And carried to Mycenæ, to the Gate of Lions.

Now they look on dead Eurythion, and form their ranks;
The troop of Centaurs clatter from the tented shade,
From clouds of the hillside to the chestnut land
Of valleys, soft swelling to their smooth, firm breasts,
As ripe a battleground as Hippodamia's hills,
Where died Eurythion, breathing from her lips;
Yellow was the cornland as her waist of amber,
With tassels of the chestnut for her saffron curls.

The true Hippodamia sees the Centaurs die,
One, and then another, and she smiles at this
While proud Pirithous musters the Lapithæ:
They divide, they run with orders: the Hero Theseus,
And Hercules, giant herdsman, are captains of the van

BATTLES OF THE CENTAURS

Marching in the summer land, along the corn;
Pirithous, in rear of them, waiting for his time,
Halts with the mainguard: the trumpets sound for battle:
All the Lapithæ, every Hero marches.

A Centaur shows himself, calling with cupped hands,
On a bare hill; higher than the height of man
His voice comes down; and he shouts, but no one answers him,
And calls, calls again, into his conch of fingers,
In deep laid stratagem, lingering to be taken,
For the sides fill with Centaurs. All their troop of horse
Come up to the sky out of the hidden meadow,
Above the panting Lapithæ; they hold huge stones
High in their hands, as high as men on horseback,
And hurl them down the hillside.

But the Heroes close the double horns upon them:
The wings march in: they gather on each flank,
Surround the hills of Centaurs, but the troop has fled,
There is only spring air upon the empty hilltop
And its sight of Arcadia beyond the snows.

While Neptune kisses Ceres, and Hippodamia, missed,
Is called on every wind!
                    O where is Hippodamia?
Is she a prisoner, hidden in the summer?
But wind spells no words, the very groves are mute.

But the Centaurs drew their bows, and many Lapithæ
Felt the feathered arrows and, swan-like, from swan feathers
Sank back on the water, and in ghostly pallor
Floated their souls away upon the stream.

The Heroes march to save them:
>By laurel and by myrtle,
By leaves of sweet odour, when the fingers press them,
Sent forth, at other times, as sighings on the wind:
Man-high their shade and bruised by the shoulders,
Of bronze to myrtle bough, of aromatic breath
Shed forth as they march, who, coming on the Centaurs,
Turn the whole battle in the river bed,
Hiding in the boulders.
>Half the race of Centaurs
Perish with arrows: the Lapithæ rally:

And Theseus kills his Centaur: and Pirithous, appeased,
Spares a young Centaur, but has no quarter for the grown,
Remembers Hippodamia, and kills the youth,
Taking that life just given him again,
In no pity for his breathing all the world once more
With its scent in his nostrils, as he sniffed the morning
Standing in the cave mouth, a morning he remembered.
The moon still burned and the Centaur left his love
For a breath of sweet dawn, and watched the waning moon
Go wan and hide. Was it the pallid spectre,
The Centauress, his mother, whom he loved no more,
Deserted for the daylight, for the warmth of life,
His first true love upon the fields and in the cave,
With locks like clover curls, the hue of day
Where noon is brightest, where its wires are gold?
So mother love dies and so the other love comes after,
So day follows night, so at the door of death
Life is on our lips and we walk among our loves,
Living in their glances; but Pirithous gives him peace.
So fell the Centaurs, one and then another
Choked with the sword, while "Hippodamia," hidden,
Echoed in the woods, against the ilex walls.

Mothers of the Centaurs! Look down upon your sons!
They die. They perish. The Centaur blood is finished.
Look down from the clouds for they were born of them.

Heroes and Lapithæ rattle in that wind
In armour of metal, darker than ilex
Beside the lit chestnut with its flaming candles;
They search every glade for Hippodamia, lost,
And hear no sound, but find the print of hooves
Deep on the moss, and deeper from their load
Of Hippodamia, lifted by the stallion;
It is his vengeance and Pirithous, alone,
Goes sword in hand among the lengthening shades.

Dead, dead the darkness, starless, of no moon:
And here lay Hippodamia on the hoof marked moss,
Ringed with that crescent moon a myriad times,
In faunal emblem.
     Her living pallor
But made more real by her open lips,
Red with blood, as with all her blood,
More lovely, in death, than nectarine alive;
For this was her marriage bed, Pirithous saw her
With amber skin dying, all ripeness still
Of smoky amber, of the nectarine,
As the Centaur killed her, bleeding from his arrow,
With her lovely neck, and all her beauty drawn
To her red, red lips. Her saffron locks
Combed by his fingers, twined for her to die:
Dead before he found her: and her Centaur fled
To safe Arcadia beyond the snows.

The Farnese Hercules
(From the statue at Naples)

Heroes out of music born
March their glittering shades down myrtle alleys in the
    poet's wood
Breaking the rhymed lights of reason:
For these three lines of preface
The black cape of magic hides my head and hands
Till I fix the staring camera eye:
"Keep that position, gentlemen! keep it and look pleasant!"
The chattering agora, sudden camp of stalls,
Reaches to the statue's feet, to the platform for these stylites,
Who stand all day and night in rain's blue cage,
Fed with this water and the yellow bread of sun.

"It will make a very pretty water colour.
Look how still he keeps. Tie your sandal to his ankle."
He was among a whole white wood of statues
In the market place along a road of triumph,
Then moved with pulleys at the trumpet's sound
To the Baths of Caracalla where the rhymed lights of poetry
Bore the new Prometheus from the womb of that dead
    music.
Hercules lay broken in the heaped, dried dust;
His legs took twenty long years to find
So bitter had his fall been. To the roll of thunder
Fell he, or the red Goth's hand?

Now his dwelling is a dark museum,
A dingy hotel dining room with no food ever served,
We'll forget that dreary future for his laboured past;

THE FARNESE HERCULES

We will take him from the Thermæ to his native land,
To the poplars and the caverns, to the hills of wild thyme,
Their limestone worn by rain's slow tide
In spires and guttering pinnacles;
No foot climbs to those towers but the bearded goat
Cropping the cold herb among the cactus swords,
While winds of prophecy in hollow caves foment
To break from the shepherd's lips, or speak by signs.

The agora, that platform for the quack and the actor,
For anyone swollen with the wind of talk,
Grew to a parliament of all the muses,
Till poetry and music, spawn of words, were born
And gods walked in the harvest, or among the grapes,
To choose a mirror of themselves in men;
They tired of immortal love and stole into the harvest
Hidden in wind's raiment, or at a tower of stone
Fell in a gold shower like sun with rain;
Such were the loves of gods who schemed in green barley
To snare the bowed reapers, or grape gatherers on their ladders.

This talking, ceaseless talking, like a rookery in the elm's green roofs,
Cawed and chattered whilst they built with twigs,
Though here in the agora the twigs were beams of marble
And they worked like the rooks do by tradition and proportion;
Their temples were a shepherd's hut magnified
With ninepin pillars and a tilted roof
Walling in this open way a dark inner mystery.
Since the gods made a mirror of themselves in men,
Sculpture, a shepherd's craft—they carve in their waste hours—

Copied like a camera this echoed immortality
And matched the mortal limbs of man against the deathless gods.

Then, the forests of white statues grew
And the gods and men among them only differed in their emblems;
The athlete oiled and slippery for wrestling
Stands by a god who treads the windy hills,
You could see this naked athlete in the stadium
And hear that god speaking in the groves of philosophy,
His limbs gleaming white from sharp edges of the myrtles
In the fainting sunset when the lengthened shades are lifted;
Then were those arsenals of legend stored,
The hills of thyme were the stepping stones to heaven
And the wind spake in oracles from sacred woods.

The normal, the simple life was in the young, fresh air
With the shepherds sitting by their sticks of fire
Or the fisherman living by his nets of fortune
Throwing for fast silver in that tideless sea.
It was the Golden Age before the Age of Gold began;
How snow soft were those legends falling every year
In a winter of white blossoms through the speaking trees,
For they formed, like the snow does, to the shapes they loved,
To a sliding gentle poetry that is made of nothing,
Though it lives by the body of its melted beauty,
In a sharp, deep river, or at a fountain in the rock.

The tumbrils slowly creaking under pyramids of grapes
That ran down their life blood on these boards and on the oxen
Took home the husbandmen,

Maddened by these fumes and by the pulsing sun;
This shadow life of drunkenness, this mocking of the fire of health,
Gave birth with its mirror to a world of ghosts,
The theatre and its actors began at that stained trestle
And masks to keep the mirror truth and hide the living difference
Were born in that blue autumn. The mock children
Of fine shepherds and their bearded goats were shown;
And the goat god in dark rocks once seen.

Where the tumbril waited in the pinetree shade
They made a trodden dancing floor,
This grew into a half-moon of rough-hewn stone,
To the theatre of mock death and laughter;
There did these ghosts stalk on stilt-like pattens
And thunder the heroic verse through mouths of brass.
In the dun twilight other shadows creep,
While this first giant art is born out of rolling high speeches;
Other shadows creep between the syllables
In chequers so that light or shade can hide them,
And Harlequin's wand becomes a thyrsus in the grape harvest.

Thus was the camera eye tricked and cheated,
For these ghosts with their masks and stilts were outside life.
Was ever death so cold as this, or love so fiery?
Those armoured gods, those women calm as oxen,
In the cold heroic mazes, in sacred families of tragedy,
Move to their destiny. The beardless ephebus
Comes through the flower thickets, stands naked in full light of day,
For he was the vehicle of their strange loves;
So to those legends we have giant stilted shades,

Ox-eyed women, and young naked limbs
That will tear on a rose bush, or stain with the grape.

He was born, our Hercules, in the yard of a stone mason,
Dragged in his matrix by a team of oxen
And tilted with a lever to that ground thick with statues,
There he stands rough and clumsy like a boy on his first school day
Waiting for the chisel and the cold eye to study him.
Tie your sandal to his ankle! Tease him like a bear!
Though who can the Gypsy be who leads him, ring in nose,
By green hedges, his rough bed at night,
To the crowded, noisy agora,
To that theatre where the Gypsy's horn
Sounds among the shadows that the statues throw?

Twelve labours, twelve slow tours on foot,
Has He who made the beetle walk laid out before him,
Though the labours of Hercules are tasks he can't avoid,
He is carried there by instinct like dogs to a dog fight.
Instinct, little voice, scarce seen, scarce felt,
Like the Indian on his elephant who guides it with a whisper
And can ride in a castle on that patient wave back
Through green waters of the Indian bright boughs;
So, turned Gypsy to our Hercules
We will walk in the dew deep orchard
Tasting apples of Hesperides.

Tie your sandal to his ankle! He will be your winged Mercury
To run before you. Won't he move? Won't he stir?
He is dank, cold, and dewy like mushrooms of the night
Spawned in summer showers from goatskins of the rain;
He leans on his truncheon like a great policeman.

THE FARNESE HERCULES

Glycon was his sculptor, and Lysippus before him
Had planned this demi-god leaning weary on his club;
Lysippus of Sicyon with his fifteen hundred shapes of stone
Who wrought his white nightmares like the sculptors of Carrara
From the salt white quarries;—
While Glycon had the Romans for his Yankee patrons.

At least there was never such a gladiator:—
Or there'd be no audience in the Roman theatre;
He'd eat them up like paper!
No hero on wars of love in the wood's green tent
Ever heard the nightingales, bright stars to such an armour;
Had he lulled, my Hercules, below these lights
That sang in wan air
Before the moon in green tree windows,
The glitter, while he slept, that should have touched his steel
Would lie on no armour but his heaped rings of muscle,
Rocks deep hidden in a sea of smooth skin.

He should be the sentinel on cyclopean walls
Guarding a megalithic rock-hewn town
And moved to ram's horn trumpet, blown
At the tomb mouth lintel of that city gate;
He is watching the flocks of sheep, dropped petals from the clouds
That move with shadow stilts along the hills' green sides,
Or he guards the hayricks, honeystacks of grass,
That are pitched like a shepherd's hut with high, sloped roof
And yet are combs of honey that are cut for the cattle,
For they store all the yellow light that fed the grass
And hold sun and rain within their golden straws.

These villages of giant stone spread like a fashion
From mouth to mouth of shepherds
As by beacons on high, lonely hills;
Temples like giant hearthstones are built on the bare plains
And they save up their captives for the sacrifice of fire
When they burn a wicker tower of them above the stones.
That was a Golden Age for Hercules,
On wrestling ground, or at rough bed of leaves,
In fleecy nights of winter
Wrapped in woven wool as white as they,
When breath turns to smoke.

See him throw stones to keep the rooks off the barley!
They start quite low and rise on a parabola,
They blossom at their zenith, shut their wings into a meteor,
And fall like an anchor out of the clouds among the rooks.
See him run to turn the drove of horses!
He can blow in a corner of the barley
And bend that sunny hair against the wind,
So the reaper with his sickle cuts two sheaves for one;
Those horses that he turned and headed
Gallop in front of Hercules like a drum shower of the rain
Falling on loud leaves and the thatched hair of houses.

Hercules as husbandman is in the grapes,
He pulls the blue bunches from their roof of leaves
To fill the wicker baskets that the women hold
And they spill them into a pyramid in a space between the vines:
It towers like a summer wave full of the sun,
Could this be still and frozen for a word to break;
Then into that deep sea of sun and summer rain
He wades and treads until its fire is loosed;

THE FARNESE HERCULES

The rocks and hollow hills echo with his laughter,
Rocks that are the cold bed for goat foot gods,
And caves, old mirrors for their sighs and loves.

The kneeling, fainting cherry trees,
So deep their green sails and their mouths of fire
That they burn like a galleon to the water line,
Kiss with red lips his hands
That feel among the apple trees
To their branches heavy with those sweets of rain.
Who knows what voices rang among the boughs
When limbs, so light they were like wind between the leaves,
Climbed from cool water,
And the orchard, one green tree of birds,
Sang from every window in its sunny leaves?

Cunning or big muscle were the ways to power,
To the Emperor lifted on a shield in the camp,
Till the Hebrew prophet and the fishermen;—
Then the men of destiny like old idols were thrown down
And the trumpets of triumph became horns at the tournament;
The walls of the castle like white cliffs of chalk
Stood like bulwarks to the green sea of time:
Long Gothic faces of the fair haired warriors
Showed from beetle armour for those glitters down the myrtle glade:
Those ancient heroes to long trees of birth
Surrendered, and the herald's horns.

Now there'd be no use for him, no work for Hercules,
Unless he turned policeman
And joined the Irish bullies on loud Broadway;

He could part the streams of traffic with a white-gloved hand
And snare the gunmen in their stolen motor;
Glycon and Lysippus would be sad to see him
With his fugal muscles in neat armour of blue cloth.
Away with him! Roll him to the drab museum,
To the stone companionship of other shades:
Let there be a banquet of the gods
On tired air through tangled, cobweb windows!

He lives again in thin shade of the olive trees
At a cold fountain in the rocks
Watering his oxen;
From the orchard walled with river stones
Apples of sweet rain hang forth
While kneeling, fainting cherry trees bleed fire on to the grass:
Let those green wings of the wind, sharp leaves,
Give him music for his feasting,
While fine nymphs of the river from their sighing brakes
Climb into the orchard, where great Hercules
Sleeps by sweet rain boughs and by cherry mouths of fire.

Fragment from *Bohemund, Prince of Antioch*

BOHEMUND, give us Bohemund, and take back time;
O raise him from the porphyry,
Lift the porphyry coffin lid: we'll look inside!
Bones and dust of Bohemund, shreds of his purple,
The big bones of Bohemund, his big, bare bones,
Knockkneed and huddled, hurried to the tomb.
O close down the porphyry: we'll let him lie!
Nine hundred years old, nine centuries asleep:

FRAGMENT FROM BOHEMUND

Bohemund, give us Bohemund! Blow down the horn,
Wind the horn once more, and once again, for him:
He comes up from the porphyry, alive and fresh,
To tell us of his hunting in the ilex wood,
In a Syrian valley, up among the hills,
Near the spreading cedars and their crocus lawns.

It was his paradise to listen down the wind,
With brooded falcon waiting on his wrist:
The grass was all flowers to his horse's hooves,
Pied, white and yellow, with blue candles burning:
And taller, blue lilies, little carillons
Strung on green stems, the lilies of the valley
Shaking their bells and silvering the vale
With breaths of innocence, in little sighs:
A wood of anemone: and lifting on the wind
White cups of peonies, like globes of snow
Held in a hand and patterned to the fingers,
Most lovely of hands, for all those hearts of snow
Were hollow where the heat was, as though that hand
Worked from its own heart, and, suffering there,
Left its sad thoughts to blossom on the wind,
Waiting what befell—until the petals fall.
And no one came, no lips spoke,
Only in the boughs
The ringdove crooned,
And the falcon, impatient, tried to spread his wings
Till the hood was slipped.

He flew to kill the turtledove,
In Indian peace, in Himalayan calm,
Crooning in its Caucasus, its lands of flowers,
To towers of roses, cities of the petal
Bright as fires of sunrise and as many hued,

The India of its slumber, in our cooler summer
Dreaming of its winter where it fled our snows;
And frightened the turtledove and took it on the wing,
When Bohemund rode up through the trumpet flowers
Content to be the death of it, to stop its song.
O this was his India, he walked in it
In a jewelled forest in Golconda's caves
Of branching pillars, down to Coromandel
The coast of pearls and by a strait of sea
To shores of amber, every step he took
Treading on wonders.
                O trumpets of the battle,
Blow loud for Bohemund and bring him back
To the great Crusade, the chivalric march,
Gathered in the green North, among the meadows.
Loud bells proclaim it in a fiery tocsin,
The fanatic preaches, screaming in his rags
And calls for blood in hatred of mankind
Hurling all to death, to universal slaughter;
Sharp stones tortured him, and pricking of the briars
In the thorny wilderness around his cell,
The cold stone walls, the damp breath of the cavern,
His long years in prison and the long hard nights.

Hatred gives him holiness, his hermit rage
Calls them by the tocsin and the march begins
Through the plain to the snowy Alps,
And to Italian coasts where luxury and calm
Have tamed the Northmen, where they live in ease
In richest honeycombs of cedar and of cypress,
All stained with gold, and from the mulberry trees,
From lands of cloves and spices, in soft webs of silk
Belie their armour; but the trumpets and the drums
Break their satrap slumber and they rise to arms,

FRAGMENT FROM BOHEMUND

Bohemund among them, who in the softer East
Battles like a dæmon, then for satrap pleasures
Repairs to Lebanon, where, with her snows
He tempers the hotter fruit, and for his wine
Sends for goatskins of Sicilian slopes,
Terraced in sulphur and the heart of lava
To the faunal ilex, high as ilex grows
Below the oak woods, far below the snows
On Etna's mountain with her mouth of fire:
Sends for wine of Etna, and in Lebanon's sweet woods,
Near his city, Antioch, upon the crocus lawns,
Drinks the wine with snow, and in a silken robe
With turbaned servants and a shadow from the South,
Of porphyry, or basalt, to hold his heavy arms,
Rides forth for hawking with the bird upon his wrist
And fights no more battles, but effete with ease
Wages mimic war within the hollow woods
And to Saladin's first trumpet goes from Antioch,
Back to paler Italy, and dies, disgraced.

Where Tancred, and Conradin, and Manfred lived,
In the Paladin kingdom,
They bury him with honour:
Bohemund, only Bohemund, has kept his tomb,
Is dust in it, and has his name carved there
To wall in his privacy, his shreds of purple:
But Bohemund of Antioch, the marionette,
Shines in silver armour
And, every evening plays
To coral fishers and to drunken sailors,
Among the Paladins, his giant brothers.
Happy, happy Bohemund, thus kept alive,
Called out, falsetto, by a maiden's lips
To last with the Paladins through livelong battle!

O happy, happy Bohemund, it is not death:
You are not dead, or never, never lived;
This is your life, in armour on the stage,
Playing Ariosto to the coralfishers!
Happy, happy Bohemund, you are not dead!

GROUP VII

The People's Palace

Trumpets

Woven from the tangled hair of comets
   On the never ceasing shuttles of the wind,
Night, thick Tabernacle for the sun, is pitched;
And from the deepening gloom
Ring out the trumpets,
Red and quick as sparks
Before the vivifying camp fire of the Gods.
The blare of a Trumpet is brazen, fierce
As the culminate charge that decides a battle.—
Great plumes, like clouds wind riven,
Float behind each fighter,
And their armour glints and gleams in the Sun.—
The horses' hooves beat loud, insistent,
As ominous and dire as kettledrums;
The whole Earth's expectant;
And the fields stretch green metallic
As the leaden plated sky;—far off
Small windows, kissed by the Sun's red lips,
Send back a shuddering echo,
To the blare of trumpets.
The cottage smoke, so stiff and regular,
Goes creaking through the painted air;
And everything is waiting,
Watching in uncertainty.

Outskirts

THE gold voice of the sunset was most clearly in the air
As I wandered through the outskirts of the town.

And here disposed upon the grass, I see
Confetti-thick the amorous couples—
What thoughts, what scenes, evoke, evaporate
In leaden minds like theirs?
Can I create them? These things
Which mean the happiness of multitudes?
A river bank, grass for a dancing floor,
The concertina's wail, and then the darkening day.
Raise your eyes from ground to trees
And see them stretch elastically
Tall and taller—then look along
The bank, all frayed, of the canal
Where we are sitting—the water
Lies like a sword
With marks of rust
Where the sun has caught it.

Lie back and listen:
Watch the reflections.
You see the ripples run among the leaves,
Brush them aside, like painted birds
That sing within the lattices
The sun's hot bars make with the branches.
In China I am told, my dear,
The temples are outlined with bells
That swing in the wind, or clash
Beneath the rain showers;

So when these ripples play among the trees,
Or any insect drops upon the water,
The rings and circles spread,
Make the whole trees shiver,
And far down you hear
Clash upon clash, the ringing
Of the bells that jangle with the leaves.

You cannot pierce those distances?
Look up! Look up!
Night is slowly coming to fill the valleys,
Drench the hills, and free us
From the suffocation of the sunset.
On lands all turbulent with heat
The small white houses dancing
On the rim of the horizon—like aproned children
In a schoolyard—are stilled.
The far-off hills stand solitary,
Made yellow by the sun.
Beneath them, where the river winds,
You hear the spirting of a gramophone—
A fountain playing with discoloured water;
And the strumming of a piano,
Too far for voice to carry,
Jerks like a mote before our eyes.
For all the instruments men make
Play on a public holiday,
That birdlike we may play upon a reed,
Or let a nightingale we've made
Sing among our trees of sentiment.

December 31st, 1917.

"Psittacus Eois Imitatrix Ales ab Indis" (Ovid)

THE parrot's voice snaps out—
No good to contradict—
What he says he'll say again:
Dry facts, dry biscuits.

His voice, and vivid colours
Of his breast and wings,
Are immemoriably old;
Old dowagers dressed in crimpèd satin
Boxed in their rooms
Like specimens beneath a glass,
Inviolate—and never changing,
Their memory of emotions dead;
The ardour of their summers
Sprayed like camphor
On their silken parasols
Intissued in a cupboard.
Reflective, but with never a new thought,
The parrot sways upon his ivory perch—
Then gravely turns a somersault
Through rings nailed in the roof—
Much as the sun performs his antics
As he climbs the aerial bridge
We only see
Through crystal prisms in a falling rain.

March 1st, 1918.

Pindar[1]

PINDAR asleep beneath the planes.
Then every Zephyr shook his shoulder,
Struck the pale disks,
Sent silver showers beneath the moon
To clothe his young tired body
With those pallid leaves.

And Pan let from his shuttered hive
The snub nosed honey bees escape—
A whirr of sound, throb, flutter,
Feather flight of birds,
And on the poet's lips
The swarm descends to suck his breath.

Now Pan has learnt his song
And sings it on the mountains,
The centaurs gurgling the honeyed waters
Take hand from lips, retire to caves;
Each satyr, ev'ry grape gatherer
Can hear their panick'd rumblings.

Now the song lulls; centaurs breathe again—
To daylight—sniff around; then gallop down the hills
Beneath the cliffs, poor fishermen
Hear thunder thudding of the hooves, and sail for sea,
They think a hissing thunderbolt will fall about their heads.

[1] There are two legends of Pindar. One tells how when he was asleep in a wood, whilst quite a baby, a swarm of bees settled on his lips. The other describes how Pan stole Pindar's song, and sang it on the mountains. In this poem these two incongruous elements have been combined.

And from the cliffs the centaurs hear
Flutes, like bird flights through the air,
All regular, then flurry of the wings
As breath fails in the player—
And fevered pluckings at a harp
Are birds, beneath a canopy of leaves,

Who preen their feathers, strike their beaks
Upon each quill, re-echoing
With air born ecstasy—
Could one imprison fire within a pipe of glass
To catch the surge and shrinkage of its flames,
I think we'd have in one small pipe,

A man could play on,
Every plunge through chasms where the winds play,
Through bell clear ringing rounds of rain,
Through painted distances aloof as dreams,
And every beat their wings make on clouds
Reverberant as caverns.

And with these flute sounds came the floundering
Of horns that play among the waves
Like porpoises who roll
Against the stiffened backs of water
That the waves flap,
When they break sonorously.

They say that every sound upon the earth
Is mirrored, echoed, in the upper air
And never dies; so when the sounds
The centaurs heard from passing galleys
Were washing like young tides
Among the clashing cymbals we call stars—

They broke in foam against the songs
The sirens sang, and the stifled cry
Of Sappho falling to her death—
And still there rose the lyre strung voice
Of Pindar fresh, and honey sweet,
Rejuvenate in spite of Pan.

February 11th, 1918.

Brighton Pier

How even, flat and similar,
These strips of plank beneath our feet.
Unconscious quite, my weary eyes
Force me to tread on every joint
Of plank to plank.
I seem to lay my road
Treading flat the boarding as I go—
And so I ponder,
Think still further, further, from me.
Then thump, thump, thump,
These leaden feet tread on my mind
And bring me back again.
Strips of white trouser
Shooting to and fro,
Jumping forward, jerking back,
Gay blazers, skirts of flimsy muslin,
Squirts of sunshine, flopping hats—
The planks re-echoing and springing to the footsteps.
Here, at the water's edge, I stop.
And lean upon the parapet:—

There are pierrots dancing in their booth
Flooded with strong draughts of sunlight;
They twist and turn beneath the rays
Like wisps of faint blue smoke.
I cannot hear their song:
But distant sounds
Like bubbles breaking
Reach my ears.—
Small waves roll gently forward,
Raise their tired heads
And slowly break to foam—
As sudden as you turn
A page over in a book.

Li-Tai-Pé

(He strolls in the garden after dinner.)

Full moon fruit hanging on the orchard tree
Wind shakes them—clash of calabashes
Full peal of bells—each fruit
A honey hearted rain drop
Falls pattering on the straight ribbed leaves.

I move my eyes, then look around
Can hear the frostflowers raise their heads
In ev'ry dewdrop I have crushed—
Far back my sinuous footmarks stretch—curved snail walk.

Then wink my eyes
Ah! only one moon, and that

As large and round and heavy as an egg—
In branching clouds—the Phœnix nest it is!
With half-fledged Phœnix young.

Their song now swims upon the air
Like painted ships that plough the sea.
The wind puffs play among the weeds—
Tree tops tremble—temple bells clank in the wind—
All flute sounds in the Phœnix throat.

June, 1916.

The Moon

THE white nightingale is hidden in the branches
 And heavy leafage of the clouds.
She pours down her song—
Cascades threaded like pearls,
And the winds, her many noted flutes
Flood forth their harmony—
But the Earth turns away
Swinging in its air and water rocked cradle.

Tahiti

WHEN the hood of night comes on the land
 My ship is rocked by the sunset wind—
Shrill voices from the town
Cleave the air like darts;
When they sing in chorus
It were as if steel arrows of the day,
The showers of rain, rebounded to the dome of air.

When one alone shouts loud, his jaggèd voice
Blares like a trumpet. Banjos and drums
Beat, twang, and throb hysterically
Outside the mud built huts.

Far off, the sun, caught spider-like
In its cloud web, is seething down the sea
And churns the waves, spatters them with blood.
Despairingly it waves red tentacles, clutching
Fiercely each wool white wave crest, then splutters out—
Ashore, the tall trees flap their foliage,
Cut out like stage trees carved in canvas.
The leaves whip the trees as ropes flick the masts
Of every salt fed ship;
Then the hood of night comes down, and from the shore
The Babel grows.
     —I dream that I, too, sing—
Lanterns are lit—great stairs of light
Shake in the water;
All dank and wet I seem to climb,
Swaying on soundless gold—so silently
Above the land, into the distant moon,
Alone, and ringing clear as a bell.
It is a gong, beaten by the drunkard clouds
Which reel on the horizon, and by the echoing laughter of
 the stars.
—Even the sound dies now, and the white bubble,
Drop of milk, seems to feed
And love whole worlds, turning gold to silver,
All ugliness to beauty.

Barrel Organs

1. *Prelude*

River-like, this cold quick wind
Swirls and eddies down the street.

In the wide level of the sounding sea
Sudden pitfalls gape:
Deep laid traps for ships:
Great seething hollows, mirrors for the sky:
Blue deep chasms, flecked with red and gold,
Blown with foam, and live
With salt stiff't sails and sailors' bodies,
Golden treasures and forsaken ships—
And in these hungry seething deeps there lies
The fleeting wild reflection of the skies.

So, in the steady flow of wind
That swirls and eddies down the street,
All sense and sight
All sound and sorrow
Resolve around us here:—
Fly straight as arrows to this spot
And fall around us—
The jaggèd stones are live with sound,
And one can hear the shuffling feet on them
Tread low, monotonous, inevitable—
Vast armies marching down the corridors of Time.
Oh! how this music throbs
And lifts our bodies from the street!

Squat chimneys rattle and revolve
And you can hear
The weathercocks fly helterskelter.
Tall drink shops with bedizened fronts
Decked out with golden letters;
Inside them voices raised in quarrel
Seem in an instant to jump nearer
For the swing doors with frosted glass,
And bars so thick they seem to guard a treasure
(Not screen drab ugly drink),
Fly open with a squirt of yellow light
Which only shews with emphasis
The dust and crumbling paper in the gutter.
A love sick ballad with a chorus,
The snarl and tin tongued tremolo of tenors,
With mellow, even toned basses,
Make the blind and beer-daft beggars
Stamp their feet and swing their arms in unison,
So they forget the cold and hungry vigil for a ha'pence.
The doors swing to, and there is no more light.
The darkness throbs around one like the pulse
Within a frightened animal.

On either side stretch archways,
Deep like sleep and hopeless as the sea.—
A drunkard shuffling his slipshod feet
Towards his dreary starving home,
Sings in an even yellow voice:
Sings of pleasures he has never tasted,
But sings with full conviction.
The shop signs creak and rattle in the wind
And from far-off a clock strikes (half-heartedly).
The passage of the hours is uniform;
They glide together like the tapping of a drum—

Our lives are but as sand within the hour-glass:
One half is up, the other down;
So, like the ever shifting sea,
Devouring misery eats up
All the inroads of prosperity—
Just as the fangs of seething foam,
Which race and slide o'er the tawny sand,
Are quick withdrawn by the immutable tides.—
The moon, young light haired shepherd
Has but to lead away his star fed flocks,
The wool white foaming breakers of the sea,
Then pasture them again;—
And when he rests behind those thyme clad hills, the clouds,
To see the homing stars, striped honey bees,
And shuns the sun god's ravenous embrace,
Without a sight of him, the dragon writhing foam
To the gentle piping of his wind stopped flute
Draws back again—
    Our lives are short,
And do we differ but by our degrees of misery.
We have a solace.—Listen then:

2. *The Feathered Hat*

OH! how this music throbs and lifts our feet!
That day the sky was molten gold,
The wide fresh smelling Earth was dancing
Beneath the glittering sun shafts—
One side, the street was dark,
As deep and cool as water wells,
The other was ablaze with light:—

Great bars, feet thick, shot down
Between the Sun's hot eyelashes;
Motors with their rush and whirr
Shot into heated glamour, then came
Black and dull, alternately.
Between these blazing shafts of heat.
The organ plays a slow and measured waltz.
I had my best hat with the feather in it;
My boots were thick with dust,
I held up my skirt and swayed,
Could not dance, the heat was such.
I moved so slow, grew tired and more tired,—
Could think of nothing,
      Then of a sudden came the syncopation;
It seemed to clutch my heart,
My nerves came strung, like banjo strings—
I seemed to twang them with my hands and toes,
My heavy boots throbbed like catapults a-shooting!—

    Reverberate thud of thunder drops
    Shafts and chasms of blinding light
    Cavalry gallop of falling leaves
    Crackle and spark of shooting stars.

Mrs. . . . or a Lady from Babel

"Sprechen sie Deutsch? Parlez-vous Francais?
Parlate Italiano? Dearest Child!"

    Mrs. H. would float the words
    As jewels from her sunshade,

Which to my infant eyes
Seemed as the fountain of all frankincense.
Beneath the twittering shadow
She leaned out, looking in one's eyes,
Her body perfectly enmeshed
Beneath the clinging scales of gold,
And all her landau
Filled with the falling jewels—
The melting of the million bells
Set ringing when the wind breathes
And the blue spaces of the sky
Are filled with shaking leaves—
Divine wisdom as a freehold gift
From black gloved hands—
The feast of untold tongues!

On a bridge one evening
From behind the nearest house
The sunset air came suddenly alive with sound,
The throbbing from a mandoline fell forth
As the long lines of water when a boat floats by.
This ended, she was asked for coppers
In Italian.

"Coachman, drive on!
Mes meilleurs sentiments à maman,
Mes meilleurs . . ."

Week Ends

Blow your long horn,
Red cloud,
Before the wide thrown gates
And fresh lit braziers of heaven;—
To move the snowy mane
Like mist above the plain,
And thus uncover
Lawns like level seas,
And houses cool as trees
Run round by balconies
that lead from house to house
And shew the sky against
A web of shivering leaves
Struck through with gold.

    The gardener must drop his fruit
    And running down the ladder from the tree
    Must bow respectfully
    To Mrs. . . .
    Who walks into her Paradise
    Like a young deer playing in its park;—
    And I must enter as a friend
    To watch her wise commandments—

"The roses must be sprayed,
And judging from the apples in your hand
A thousand wasps have dug there."
                       "Yes, M'um."

"Yes; I think so;
And the borders are not near enough,
these stalks again are short enough,
Why aren't they longer?"
       " Yes! M'um."

" Well then, you see,
I want the treetops trimmed,
And then at tennis
One can watch the steamers
Through Lord Dodo's chimneys."
       " Exactly."
        " Yes! M'um."

" And growing in the beds,
Embroidering the paths,
Gazing in each other's eyes
Wherever there is water
I've laid geraniums
Like this one."
      " I see."
       " Yes! M'um."

" Hold it!"   " Yes! M'um."
" Whilst I show this gentleman
The way I've dug the lake
Just lying where it nets the houses
And reflects them with their window boxes."
      " Fascinating."
       " Yes! M'um."

"What do you think my husband
Waits for in the train?"

"Tell me!"
"Mum."

"Every yard the train comes
Nearer to the station
He's thinking of the view;
Steps on to the platform,
Leaves the station,
Turns the corner,
And it's there before him."

"M'um."

"A moment, m'um!
Miss Argentine was telling that her trees . . ."
　"You see it is no selfish pleasure,
Not a private toy——"
　"May I speak a moment, m'um . . ."
"Others share the joy."

That moment there came
Ringing through the leaves,
Shaking the canopies
And falling from the branches like soft snow,
The voice of some one from a balcony:

Mrs. . . . was listening
To recognize the call
That deals a deathblow to each afternoon.
With but a brief farewell
This lady left us,
And all the while
We saw her white dress

Glistening through the boughs,
And heard her footsteps
Leave the lawn
To sound upon the gravel,
Till she left a railing of gold spears between us;
While even then
We heard her answer
Mocking questions lowered through the air.

Valse Estudiantina

A WALL of cactus guards the virgin sound
Dripping through the sword edged leaves—
The wayward milking
Of your mental stalactites
On the strung bells of music,
Arrests the moment,
Petrifies the air.

As you trudge along the path
Laid down before you,
Counting all the trees,
Remembering the turnings,
Instead of resting on the wooden seats,
You lie among the thistles in the sun.
Your poor jangle spreads along the street,
Filtering the voices of the passer-by,
Embroidering the singing in the lines of wire,
And masking as with histrionic aim
The bird sound of long-distance messages.
Now with a practised hand
The music master will release the waltz

That makes a difference in our lives.
With one hand on the railing
To feel the rings of sound,
One might emphasise the vision—

Some are sitting under flame touched trees
Where the generous sun
Has run the fierce green plumes
Set quivering on the harp strings of the boughs,
Has run them to a fine fire of gold,
Has quickened them,
As islands cut the currents of the sea,
To the full spun colour
Of the floating jewels
That part the wind's gold hair,
And fill the ultimate sea
With all its canopy of clouds,
And tents of quick blue hills
With the new message of their incense cells.

Beneath these trees
The suffocated crowd extends
Its troubled surface,
Till toying with another figured shape
The extreme couples lie among the grass.
This tune brings evening ringing down
On the well-bedecked windows of the day,
And rising on their tired feet,
Running the fingers through their flower decked hair,
They leave the vast area of the band
Moving on the tight rope of the tune.

Ring out, ring out now, ring out now,
The blare of your hundred brass trumpets

Shake the leaves down, shake the leaves down,
Make the clouds dance like flowers in the wind.

In the darkening room
You sit beside the piano,
Where the music master
Stretches his shadow.
As he moves his hands,
In your mind ringing on its meals,
The rightful tunes to play
Are the sweet songs of birds,
The yaps of dogs,
Hot water tapping in the leaden pipes,—
As a final consummation
Father arriving by the evening train.

GROUP VIII

Extracts from *The Thirteenth Cæsar*

From *The Opening of the Tomb*

'Tis a pity they are ashes!
   Could we but find their bodies,
Opening the porphyry to see those sores within it,
We'd unroll the league long bandages
And rub their bones with salt:
We'd see if they have life yet—if their sores are open still;
And as the lids—those locked jaws—
We prise and lever open,
We'll treat them to a trumpet blast:—
They'll know those brazen tongues once more.
When the light breaks again for them
We must beat up their dawn into a blaze of ceremony,
Their waking sight will welcome us;
They must know we have our Cæsars still.

From *At the Bedside*

The mere act of talking blew those ashes in our faces,
   There was only dust left of him
For a pillar to his memory:
But this column on the wind hung still for a moment
As though the winds held back from it and would not wave
   their wings,

Lest these ashes from that old flame raked
Grow cool and are scattered by the soft breath of feathers:
And they waited while a voice might speak—
The soul out of this emptiness.

We all were waiting with our hats off for the flashlight,
And the screens round the coffin were to keep the winds away;
It was no use brushing us and breathing in our faces:
But the public must have its drugs,
And so I'll give the wind its feathers.

Cæsar's dust, trembling column, can be clearly seen
To the right of the photograph;
To the left the famous company
Gathered here to greet him, and to see him wake.
But he never got as far as us, he never met his peers,
He never met the masseur who would rub his limbs to life,
No more than he tasted the champagne and oxygen,
That were waiting for those crumbled lips to form again
And gape for life.

He hovered for a moment, one cruel moment, near to living,
Near enough to speak, had he but throat and tongue to mumble with;
But we reached him in time and found that brain intact;
We could read it like a tape machine and know his mind,
He spoke a clipped Latin and the rest we found in images;
It was quick work taking it,
For he was soon gone!

"I am in the soldiers' camp again
And they call out for the circus,

I am too weak still to speak to them,
My stunned head rattles, I am far away, half-sleeping,
The trumpets blow for me, to tell my coming,"
(These the fanfares that we blew beside his coffin,)—
"I shall find the soldiers ready, all lined up to listen:
Let me close my eyes and sleep again,
I will wake in a moment
And be strong enough to deal with them."
He faded out of contact, and we lost his spark of life,
Like a drowning man he sank from us
And we wondered if he'd rise again,
Where we should find him, and how to keep our hold of
    him.
He was far away,
Dreaming of such peacefulness as had been his,
Bed his only paradise,
And that a place of pain:
He was safe in his coffin like a child in a womb,
For he dreaded to be conscious
And did not want to live again:
But we reached him in time, and so he had no choice.

This was louder cockcrow than ever Cæsar heard
Blown in a fanfare, as light broke on the world
Rustling its white feathers at his open tent door:
And he stirred at the trumpet, for it patterned out his ashes,
Like wind in dead leaves scattering them:
He'd wake if he only could, he'd choose, now, to be born
    again,
But this flame that we had tended, this little soul of ashes,
Fled from us,
On plumes of wind, invisible,
It rested, not trusting to our hands,
Lying into porticoes we could not reach,

Into deepset shadow that had never heard the trumpet-tongue,
Where no voice cracked the stillness.

From *As of Old*

It is only this last century that the crack appeared,
That the mark came on the ceiling and the plaster broke,
That we came to knock the idols down
And quickly put up others:
Like burglars at a shrine
Who take the god, and leave a copy,
Safe till someone dusts it and finds out the fraud.
What subtle difference! What baser gold!
What degrees from the Hapsburg to the Corsican!
For one was pacific, cruel to criminals and heretics,
And the other, salamander, only lived in fire,
Fed on the quota, his fixed levy from humanity,
The first new minotaur in our greater, modern maze,
That monster in the dark pool stirred by us
When the waters were troubled and we would interfere—
He grew like a tree of fire, his boughs did spread,
Giving us shade, for his very shadow was a flame
Which lit space he troubled with dropping fruits of fire,
Till, in the flow of years, the core within this flame was seen,
The fire's heart smouldering,
Like coal that's cooling black again:
And his space of life, too quickly lived,
Brings him to old age too soon.
The laurels and the eagle
Were fit symbols of his Roman rule:

Like the toga of his statues,
Rightly folded, never worn by him,
Yet this was our progenitor,
The father of our modern masters,
The first man among us
To make a study of the public:
To find out what they wanted
And to make his wants their own,
By subtle persuasion, and by vaunting of his patriotism,
Shouting his own virtues till others had to copy them.
The art of proclamation he invented for his purposes,
And to this end alone it is better that a crowd can read,
For then, as they gather round to read the printed placard,
No longer is it magic that he works among them,
But they are all in his confidence
And he becomes their spokesman,
For they think that they have chosen him to work their will—
This is subtle alchemy, mutation of reality,
For the voice out of these placards—the wind among these leaves—
Orders them and moves them
Like a voice and wind from heaven;
They work with it, drinking in the words they read,
And never know their eyes are tricked
With a false mirror held to them
That can magnify some objects and diminish others.

This art we have developed
Till their eyes are like the horse's eyes,
Obedient to its master
Because it sees him twice his size.
They shall bow ten times before the idols that we carve for them,

And shall shiver like young leaves at the mention of their enemies;
If we start a fire, they'll watch it
And their breath will fan the flames.
The trumpets blown for us, to shout our honour,
Will sound so shrill to them, they'll hear no others,
They will ride in our triumph, willing captives to our stratagem,
Snared by steely mirror, and glass armour bright to look at.

GROUP IX
Serenades

1.

Sigh soft, sigh softly,
Rain thrilled leaves,
Let not your careless hands
Stem the gold wind!
Let not your greensleeves
Swim in its breath,
As water flowing;
Lest your thin hands
Make gurgle down the crystal hills
The gaudy sun's pavilions
Whence he distils those showered scents
Whose virtue all true turtles croon,
Beneath their swaying palaces,
Sing low, then, turtles,
    Sigh soft, swift wind,
        And, fountains, cease your flutings,
           Melulla, now,
                Lean on your balcony! look down!
                My strings shall sing.

2.

Open your window. Let the air flow in,
Alive with waterfalls of flashing wings,
So can your fever know a cooling touch
And feel the feathers of my song as such.

Is all silent in your room?
Then come down among the dew soft lawns,
And if I knew the stairway for your feet
Should lie below it in the luscious grass
And watch your coming, as one waits to feel
Cooler from showering of falls
That play, like you, among the burning rocks.
Then with fulness in my arms,
Ripest weight down bowed from trees
To fall through sun's heat to the green
Laughing lawns more soft than water;—
Full with ripeness, tasted, fired,
I shall journey through the heat
With my load of living fruit;
And if I do not like the lawns
Can lay it on a yielding cloud
Whose proud battlements will melt
And run, as water, at your burning touch.

3.

I SEE no breath upon the window's water,
Hear no feet below the shining trees;
Must I never let the music slacken,
Fold its wings away, sink on my knees?
Will the leaves tremble till I know their tune
In fiery praise of all the licking tongues
That lap the crystal darkest night has laid
To light her feet along the fickle walls,
Unseen, but built again when daylight comes?
In between these trembling leaves
And underneath the liquid light
Another harvest has its sheaves,

The gold heads of the foam shine bright.
Waves, as houses built on cloud,
Crumble to nothing as they sail;
The windows where you once were proud
Are raining water; fence and rail
That latticed all the roads of sight
Are twisted rainbows, broken swords.
The way is open, where you lie,
I see the clouds climb down the sky
And lay you in the frothy waves
That run to meet you, as your slaves.

Hortus Conclusus

Cherry Tree

My salamander in a world of flame,
Safe and breathing,
Come lie beneath this cherry tree,
This green shade heavy hung with coals of fire;
There is only this for coolness while the sun is high—
Zephyr in these branches could never spread his wings,
And rain will never reach us here, so close the boughs,
So dark their shadow that we hide within it—
Grow cool in this shade and then to show your skill
Act the salamander and in the fire lie still,
Let light like honey shine upon your skin:
When you're hot and like a comb of fire
Glide back into this shade,
Bend that heavy branch down with your hand upon its fruit,
Ripe cherries and a honeycomb must make my bread and wine.

Gardener's Song

"Wind, come run to help me,
  Flash your wings, I see you clearly."
I waited till he stretched them wide
Down sailing through the sparkling tide;
Now he helps me floating here.

At my side he rides above
Wherever on my work I rove,
If at a tree's foot stooping low
He sways the branches to and fro,
In green shade waiting.

When I fear the staring sun
By my ears I feel him run,
He can make me all the shadow
To hide in while I walk the meadow,
By cool air quickened.

Lawn and hill are just the same,
Cool and happy at his name,
The hanging wood which is his home
Rings with birdsongs while we roam,
Together working.

While I nurse and prune, he sows
Deft at the labour that he knows,
The seedpods with his plums to touch,
Not too soft, nor overmuch,
With wide wings scattering.

So does the seed float down the air,
While loudly shines the sun's gold hair,
And in and out the strands there fly
The floating birds who call and cry,
Their harvest reaping.

The seed, like grains of gold, they take
And for their airy roofs they make,
Where for their store they heap it high
And all the leaves and branches nigh
Ring while they glisten.

Most the wind has scattered wide
Like yellow sand for air's strong tide,
Here is my harvest that I wait,
The sunny waves run here to mate,
With the gold sand lying.

Come, wind, make me quick a shade,
For, like a bee, I rob and raid,
The offspring of this love to snare
And take their increase for my share,
In hot sun reaping.

The Red-Gold Rain

Orange Tree by Day

Sun and rain at work together
Ripened this for summer weather;
Sun gave it colour tawny red
And rain its life as though it bled;

In the long days full of fire
Its fruit will cool us when we tire.
Against the housewall does it grow
With smooth stem like a fountain's flow,
Dark are the leaves, a colder shade
Than ever rock or mountain made;
When the wind plays soft they sing,
For here the birds' songs never ring,
Quite still the fruit that in a golden shower
Will fall one day to flood this tower.

Orange Tree by Night

IF you feel for it pressing back the glossy leaves
The fruit looks cold as if its sullen fire is dying,
So red the ember that you scarcely dare to touch it:
And when your fingers close upon its moonlike rind
Chill must be the flavour like a hidden fountain
Whose waters sparkle springing clear from out the rock—
What are its leaves then, but wings, or the wind?—
Wings to hold the fruit high and cool it in the clouds,
Or wind blowing over those hot rocks that hold the water?

Damson and Medlar

THESE two keep summer in their lips
Till their slow fruit the hoar frost sips,
That mouth of winter on deep summer's mouth
Bears sweet plenty from sad drouth;
And O, their heavy towers above
Are night and day to owl and dove,

Their thick flowers shut these birds away
Though in that dark the boughs make day.

O what can sleep be in that light
Of myriad flower eyes touched with sight,
All looking for the dove's long croon,
Their sad meridian, their noon?
What dreams of other life than this
Lived in another emphasis,
Where boughs of lively coral turn
To meadows by the river's urn

Far down those fields sad conches ring
To crews of tritons winnowing,
Medlar and damson are two isles,
Two trees above the mermaid's smiles,
While knights in scaly armour ride
In scallop shells the spangled tide
By woods of crystal and of coral
That break, now, with the dove's sad moral.

So these fruits of summer flame
Hang late on their sweet gallow frame
Turned ripe with rain tears and the frost,
Most happy when they most have lost;
If tasted in the rime's white fang
They answer to the conch that rang,
And give you summer in their lips
Though their heat the hoar frost sips.

Dandelion

These lions, each by a daisy queen,
With yellow manes, and golden mien,
Keep so still for wind to start
They stare, like eyes that have no smart.
But, once they hear that shepherd pipe,
Down meadows and through orchards ripe,
They dance together, lion and daisy,
Through long midday, slow and lazy;
Each dandelion in his fierce lust
Forgets the sunset's reddy rust;
Now by night winds roughly kissed
His mane becomes a clock of mist
Which mortal breath next morn will blow,
While his white virgins bloom below.

Cowslips

Our orange wood and lemon glade
No higher than the grass is laid;
You could not walk beneath its bells
Rung heavy with the orchard smells,
But bend down to the cow's soft lip;
And see the honey lamps they sip.

These cowslips in a spring night born
Grow gentle soft and wear no thorn,
Then roll their sweetness to a ball,
The hush of breath, confining all,
Makes orange smell and lemon scent
Into a flowery parliament
Where every cowslip talks, as one,
And nothing, but that scent, is done.

Variation on a Theme by Robert Herrick

You lily beds and lily plains
  Where nothing bleeds and nothing stains,
What is your winter, when my hand
Grows heated with a lily brand?

Since a clenched handful warms me so
We'll count the miracles of snow
And see the crocus fires new lit
Shine through their lily coverlet;

This train of fire that spreads so fast
Burns out and from that winter last
The snowdrop's humble honey bell
Sighs, ghostlike, in a lily's cell.

These snowy nunneries must spoil
To help the summer's daylong toil,
Their sweet breath and sweet eyes newborn
Live in the lily-wrested morn.

Complaint

I lived through the summer while I looked for shade
But never shall I know again the ports I made,
The sail that carried me a braggart cloud,
Gone now and out of sight, a mote among a crowd,
But I walked in its sliding shade till every shadow fell.

Each day my sail into this blue sea vanished,
It carried me till nightfall and then I was banished,

I looked through all the blue night but knew I was alone
Left to count those golden heads whose hearts are stone,
Their mouths more mute than any tongueless bell.

Mute is the sun whose fire can make us blind
If we look too close upon that golden rind;
Quicker still my eyes do weep whose sight is weak
While I look upon that fiery head and wait for it to speak,
But night fell and never was this golden bell shaken.

Tomorrow I will peer again that gold lit face to find,
It will climb above the cloud I sail with, bold and kind,
But never will it speak to me, that gold bell never rings,
It lights the heavens while morning wind loud sings,
And I follow in the sliding shade, my willpower taken.

Here there is another sun with fiercer eyes
With fire more kindling for its blue disguise,
Shine then, and since your throat has power to speak,
Let me hear your singing before my tired eyes break,
I'll know I am not sleeping; I'll not fear to wake.

Warning

A GLASS gives no sure echo,
Its cavern can be dank and cold,
Swept with wind, and hung with snow.

Such is a draughty room to hire,
Whose walls are crumbling, damp, and cold,
Shut from sun, or leaves' green fire.

Water is a deeper cave
That cannot break, nor split like glass;
Here may you enter, if you're brave.

This is the hero's corded tent,
And at your shoulder there may pass
The snowy seagod with his trident.

The winds, out of those windows, sigh;
This is the cradle of the rain;
Here may you look into the sky.

The bearded stars burn cold and clear;
Here can you count their golden grain,
And snare the sun's fire without fear.

That borrowed light he lends so free
To gild the glittering branches by,
Turns to gold hair this laughing tree;

But these cool branches, one stark day
Will droop, and bow down, wearily,
All that was amber gone to clay.

That bell, that laughing tree of leaves,
Will groan with cracked note, old, and spent,
Its harvest gathered with cut sheaves.

Then will it be too late to sing;
Those crystal walls too thin a tent;
That bell tongue silent, that could ring.

The Island

Ring, gold bell, and the loud sun will laugh,
The shades creep close but they must hide tonight,
Ring in the wind until the lights are lit
And the island hung with lamps burns in its own fire
With mown grass glowing like a star's clear floor:
The isle for a stage, and the lake's low banks for audience.
Had one been but a wind one could have perched upon a bough
And shaken with a breath of air that golden hair below!
Had it, then, been the first time those blue fires burnt one,
Still deeper in the leaves my greedy wings would feel
Reaching for ripe apples at the tree's soft breast,
And when my feathers found them and I knew the fruit was ripe,
I'd look for no poison cup, but let the blue fire burn me,
Safe in this golden net with leaves for meshes.

Derbyshire Bluebells

The wood is one blue flame of love,
It trembles with the thrush and dove;
Who is this honey beacon for,
That burns this once, then never more?
Whose lutes hide in the young green leaves?
Who sorrows here when no one grieves?

The misty spaces in the boughs,
No shouts will fill, no stone will rouse,

If at those panes we beat in vain
Why hope to quench that fire with rain?
Why beat the bluebells down to find
How fire and honey are combined?

There is no space for foot to tread
Unless you bruise the flower head,
No corner where you cannot hear
The dove's long croon, the thrush sing near,
Like bells out of the trees' tall spires
These songs above the bluebell fires.

This fire of little bells, sweet eyes,
Climbs into the dove throat skies,
It shines, as here, at Bolsover
And to that Venus is a lover;
It burns in all the haunted woods
And marries with the castle's moods.

Stone Venus on her fountain ledge,
Can see above the hornbeam hedge
The only fire that climbs to her,
For sun and moon shine down on her;
And these can only reach the brim,
If they were wingèd seraphim,

Not bluebells, but bright angels' plumes,
Then burning where the sun illumes
This sharp blue fire would be her lover
And she would need no other cover,
With thrush and dove for beating heart
And bluebells hiding every part.

The casement in the castle wall
Hears the Venus fountain call,
The lutes, long dead, ring out again
And beauty like a gentle rain
Shines on each thing that has died,
Made live now with the bluebell tide.

This world of few days and few nights,
These fancies that this blue invites,
Seeks the dark, the light it shuns,
And haunts the clouded mullions,
This honey music of the spring
It winnows with the pigeon's wing.

So where deep peace should be, and quiet,
These ghosts fill with the lute's loud riot,
They hold a noisy tournament
Half-hidden in the bluebell's scent,
And Venus is but dimly seen
For lute strings and the flowers' blue screen.

We leave that mist for Renishaw
And tall elms where the rooks do caw;
But when I walk our silent woods,
Now broken with the dove's sad moods,
Not Venus, nor her lutes, I miss,
Nor find our bluebells honeyless.

Fortune

Grass, that green fire, is lit
And trees are aflame:
If we sing out loud will echo call our name?—
Echo—the answer to our heart's desire
Telling us we live with tongue of fire:
Treading the sliding shade, then, and try your voice!
I stood below the shadowed boughs
And sang out loud,
The birds, soft and crooning, did I rouse.
The leaves shook, and shook again
As struck by rain,
But every time the boughs were lifted
The shadow leaves altered,
And when I tried to follow them
My footsteps faltered.
I know not where to stand now
That same bough to shake,
I've lost the spot where echo calls
As if the hot rock spake—
Heartless stone and leaves that speak not
Answer me once more:
I search through all the trembling shade
For my footprint on your shore.
Until I find that bough I trod,
Bird quick and feather shod,
However loud I call and cry
Windless air will not reply;
I shall never know my death,
Or if I live with lasting breath—
Fortune wavers with her scales

So I'll yet try to fix my ground,
And while I sing up through the leaves
Perhaps I'll hear my echo sound.

Shadow

Shadow, Shadow,
Come to meet me
Down the hot field moving slow,
Dragging like an anchor (that white sail under),
As wind drives the clouds asunder.
Be a fountain, a jet of ice
The full leaved trees to cool;
And here, as by throw of dice
Turn the hot hill happy,
Bathe its burnings in your pool.
For smoke there must be fire,
In this room behind these windows,
Now the sun flames tire,
Let light out of the black coal break
And shadows on the four walls shake.

Shadow, Shadow,
Here you come
More swiftly running than a river's flow,
Like the green shade dancing,
Here do I lie for your surprise,
Feel the thin winds that tantalise
And know your feet advancing;
Out of the fire's heart make your spring,
Come near me, make the dark your wing;
Here, like those other ghosts, again

Till wind, my thinking, stops this rain :
Now if I shut my eyes and sleep,
Wind dies down, and clouds do weep,
But, like the fire's heart will you live,
And through the icy rain shall thrive.

GROUP X

A March Past at the Pyramids

" Two parallel straight lines can never meet."—EUCLID.

" The brotherless Heliades melt in such amber tears as these."—ANDREW MARVELL.

THE door grates open. Two wild eyes look out.
Reconnaissance. Until a readjustment
Of feathers, clothes, and gloves
Has made her ready for the street fighting.

Make way, malicious children!
Stand back, until she finishes the steps
And moves along the molten asphalt.

Throw down those cones of light
Which clothe a wall or tower!
Stand free from them, strong buildings!
As if the coat of shadows that you wear
Had fallen to your feet;
And with this gold reserve
Run down a gurgling river
Past the regimental flowers
And close cropped lawns,
As far as where the flower beds
And the pathways merge their stiff geometry
Into a simplified horizon.

The hundred handed trees
Now wave their flags against her face,

And she is sailing down the stream
Through every adverse current,
And past the threatening shoals
Of unknown residents.

The carriages across the square
Will run you down the steeper roads
And, for a slightly higher fare,
Will take you where no rust corrodes;

Along the breathless streets, that is,
Where deathless dowagers sustain
The shadow of high life in Paris,
And, in attempting it, constrain

To leash wild Nature to their funeral car,
And make the gay clouds float like kites,
And wire the tall trees, bright as stars,
For buttonholes, at awful rites.

Then why is it, that You must walk?
I see you, in imagination,
Drawn on the terraces where talk
The shades who left us with elation,

And, leaning on the carriage side,
Giants and dwarfs will point and shew
The lakes on which the satyrs ride
And hold the sails the zephyrs blow.

For in shy boats that float like birds
The satyrs once again set out
To find the fleece of golden herds,
Now feeding in the woods, to flout,

New argonauts—who now, at last,
Can see the trees, between the sails
That hang upon their golden mast;
The trees that gleam like golden rails
Are throwing the ripe fruit down,
Till, from their skiffs, the satyrs hear
The apples falling on the town
Below the clouds, as fleeces clear.

The fountains with their crystal whips
Are thrashing the teetotum dust
On which the glistening branches of the trees
Drop down a coolness as she passes.

The simplified horizon is a fixture,
It does not run before her
Like a hunted animal;
It does not leap down from the hills
And hide in the fierce green leaves
Whose lapping tongues
Drink in the rain of golden fire;
Nor swim among the waves
That spread their tails,
Shake forth their whirring wings
And try to imitate the battlemented clouds
Running against the trumpet throated wind.

Your mind is evidently set
To reach the daily goal,
The path's end,
Where you turn again
And walk back home for luncheon.
So, while you chase this mean horizon
Of blank wall, I'll follow

In your wake—a second shadow,
With more evident intention.

In this net of changing paths
And different views,
Giant figures loom like pointsmen in a fog
Setting the lines,
Directing the different phases
And future happenings,
While loud voices speak.

The man who built the pyramids
Discussing them with William Blake
Confessed the secrets of his Art,
And shewed them, once for all, as fakes.

The light wind drifting down the road
Upon the scarce heard noises of the town
Breathes just as cool upon the woods and hills.
It rests a little in the shimmering trees,
Then, while the dying sun unclasps his hair
Over the fresh fields and the gilded sea,
It plays with the swaying cornland
Through those gold moving pillars
Under the falling fountains of ripe fruit,
Till the clear evening falls upon us all.

A natural clumsiness had always been
My bar to progress
Until I conquered it by calculation;

I made a poor Narcissus
When I pored into the river,
But in its smooth black mirror

I watched the meteor acrobats,
Whose shining wings and fiery hair
Illumined the insensate air,

And in the straight lines of their flight
Among the archipelagos
That glitter like a golden rose,

I saw the roads that never meet
And on them those that never talk
Although together on their walk.

My natural clumsiness could not prevent
More abstract knowledge, and an obvious bent
For things that carry motion to a pitch
Where only calculation, with its stitch
Of make believe, and taking things for granted,
Completes the web, and leaves the answer planted
As strong as any fir tree hung with combs
To drop like bombshells at whoever comes.
My knowledge can hang nets to catch
The flaming sparks that set the thatch
Alight above the floating towers,
Trembling to whiteness under bowers
Lit suddenly, and changed to gold,
When the sun awakes and calls his fold.
And when like gleaming jewels they lie
And fill the webs with coloured sky,
I hold some in my hand like fruit,
And point to them and shew their suit
Fiery with splendour and the green
Lawns on which the proud birds preen
Feathers more gorgeous in the glow.
But leagues above the cooling flow

And running rivulets of wind,
Spanning the clouds, one foot behind
Resting upon the giant hills,
Down which the sunlight runs its rills,
The ideal pyramid will raise
Its pinnacle too proud for praise,
And, like a diamond, writes a name
Across the skies, to give me fame.

And so, while smaller men may make
The soft singing and the golden shake
With which the ripe fields greet the sun,
Into the joys for which they run
Tired lives into a broken mould,
And then renounce the joy and fold
Crippled limbs, rehearsing in their mind
Sights to remember when quick eyes go blind;
I can reach above the crowd
Without a mask, without a shroud,
And watch them counting grains of sand
To tell the height my buildings stand.

I was the man who ran along
A valley at the planet's song
And guided by the golden chain
That shone above a little plain,
I reached the folds in which there slept
The silent lambs the king had kept
Playing in the whispering air,
Until he cut their woollen hair.

Chosen as the delegate
To represent our native race,
I travelled in a caravan

Crossing hills unknown to man
Until the song died, high in air,
Which told us that our end was there.

I was the wise man of the South
And sang before the dragon's mouth
His all inevitable doom:—
And now, outside a wretched room
Fiery turbans paint the air
And Babel tongues are loosened, where
Three running streams of races meet
And lay their offerings at his feet.

Waving palm leaves toss the air
In heavy spadesful, falling where,
Like steam engines, cathedrals rise
To ring their bells within the skies.

Now who must take the precedence
Among the triple race of man
Collected at this mere pretence
To show the seeds of providence?

An African, from Mozambique,
Is ready at my right-hand side.
Will he defeat the Jewish clique
And reach there first, in righteous pride?

On a platform in the square
The local band confronts the air;
Playing together, till they sound
A note which sends the signal round.

Spontaneous gifts of homage, soon
Flooded the house and filled the road;
Late comers never knew the boon
Of bettered days, but bore the load

Unpaid and prayerless through their lives;
Wild honey, not yet in the hives,
Shall comfort those who cry alone;
Their bed the sand, their food a stone.

" Bow down!" his guardians say. " Bow down!"
Their threatening wings shut in the town;
One human tribe obeys the call;
Two others run beyond the wall.

Priority it is that counts,
However high your incense mounts.
At night the weeping stars combine
To let their golden isles outshine

The waving fire before his throne.
The springing flames obscure the groan
Of countless multitudes who pray
To painted birds, or beasts of prey.

At the vast inspiring sound
To which the tyrant god is crowned,
While the distant valleys hear
The feet of those who run in fear;

The anchorites who fill the caves
And feed with satyrs, sing aloud;
They step into the surging waves
And float to Heaven in the cloud.

The fountains with their crystal whips
Are thrashing the teetotum dust;
Mrs. X is walking in the crowd;
Mrs. Y is still outside the scrum.
Now is the daily tournament at hand
To prove the shouted statements of geometry.

The two come nearer;
Will they touch, or bow;
Or just fade back into infinity?
They are the actors in this drama;
Blind are the crowd;
Tamed Nature is an audience.
Mrs. X is ready with a smile
And spreads a feathered dignity around her;
Mrs. Y detests the common grass,
The sun scorched railings, and the folding chairs.
And so they pass, and never bow,
And Mrs. X folds up her trembling wings,
To walk back sadly through the fading day.

To show what might have been
To failing eyes;
Gold towers are building far above the sea,
And many suns are dangling in the trellises;
While little waves run in
And shake their cooling snow,
Against the shadeless sand.
The windows in the gilded towers
Have generous trees to shade them;
From their branches
Float down singing birds
To lie asleep upon the sills
Like ready instruments

Whose strings you pluck
When, through the dappled air,
Down in the jewelled orchards,
Where ripe tumbling fruit
And shimmering dew
Are dancing to the silver sound,
The Man who built the Pyramids
Advances, leading on each arm
One of the changeless parallels
That grace the cylinders of History.

GROUP XI

Two Mirror Poems

1. *On a Name Scratched upon a Window*

Deep do the letters bite that spell the name,
Though the last strokes waver as the hand grows weak
Holding firm the diamond lest it slip and fall.
Did fruit like a lodestone hang outside the window,
Or were the shining fences of the rain pitched there?
When it rains—
Like the spider's web linking leaf to leaf,
The name glitters out and links the lines of rain:
When the sun burns free—
The letters like a pattern of the frost stay on the glass.
Here, where he traced it, will the name still live
Dwelling like a mote in the eye of all who see it
As though he had fixed it in the very eye of time
Till time breaks, shattered, as a sheet of glass.
Deep do the letters bite, they mark the sky,
Till you open wide the window and the letters find their shadow
That hides in the wall until it calls out in this echo
As a cave will shout the name back in answer out of its darkness
Though all else is dead there save your rattling tongue.
The letters find their shadow and the thin echo calls to them,

Misty is the glass as though a breath had tarnished it,
For he stands once more in the window while he cuts the name,
And turning lets his hand fall, and feels the light beside him
And in that moment, till echo answers emptily,
The name becomes the body for as long as time stands still.

2. *The Poet and the Mirror*

Something of a soldier is each poet;
At least both share like triumph in their dreams,
Though poetry comes quicker than a plan of battle,
And it blows through shriller trumpets for attack.
After the sharp rivers that run down like swords,
The hills, and the baffling clouds men hide behind,
Victory, when it comes at last,
Through the veins of these two races runs the same,
They are lifted and stand still like eagles in the wind;
For both there should be halls made ready for their feasting
Filled with the false sunlight that burns pale by morning
And loud with music, though the throbbing music dies,
And nothing now is left of it,
For the poet, like music and the lights, dies back again.
How can the poet live and feast through time?
For only the soldier gets the spoil to take away.
Poor are all poets born beneath the starrèd shade,
They must live and while their days last
The showering gold may comfort them,
Sun by day and moon by night

Their purse and bread,
While grass grows to sleep on and the leaves will give them shade:
They may stand long in the cold snow with stars for crumbs,
Rain will give them water, and the light from houses warm them
As they stand outside.
Cold does the wind blow, neck deep do they wade in it,
While the pavers stretch their icy plain beneath the feet.
This is his campaigning and its flags wave on the chilled air,
That air through which his words go, from which his words are made,
While out of that thin substance, though he dies, yet do his thoughts live.
All brave soldiers, though they die, are not remembered
And so it is with poets however high they climb to die:
How, then, can his memory live who had not strength to win his battle,
Who shivered in the snow, and in the sun was parched and thirsty?
No one will remember him, himself his only friend
And all the tears that fall but his own brackish sorrow.
If no one will remember me, somehow I will make a mote
That smarts however strong the eyes
And lodges there like dust to tingle,
Living in their vision like the fire heart in all smoke,
And so each time they look
My mote smarts and they rub their eyes:
Deep as the deepest sea, unruffled, never cut by wind,
This mirror is the water where I write my name,
Eating earth up inch by inch
As the tides do, tilting at us out of the salt sea.

I stand before this mirror and I walk away,
While my image, like the dying tide, ebbs before its change:
It walks out of the mirror as though I climbed out of the water,
But yet it never ruffles and I hear no lapping waves:
These waters like the Dead Sea
Keep us floating though we cannot swim.

GROUP XII

Part II from *New Water Music*

Black faces by the crystal water born,
At the black breast clinging like fire to the dark coal,
By the clear spring born because the trees give shade,
Like ghosts, the shells of men, so quiet they are,
Wait for the bidding,
For now they feast together, while the galleon lies ready,
Its sails, like the lovers' tent for them to lie in,
Pitched on those blue fields in sighing wind
To the spiced isles blowing them.
Black faces and white sails the powers they work with,
By dark hands lifted, or running with those wide-stretched wings,
Black shade, fierce light, both serving them.
This empty shell of building, loaded with no gilding,
Lit with yellow sundust or the starry whorls of torches,
Is hung with heavy curtains in its porticoes
That lie still and listen for the dawn wind to blow;
Now they hang heavy and their folds lie still:
Cold night, cold night, made chillier by the water glitter
Though the two who feast here have the sun's fire in their veins,
In fierce rivers burning,
And every time they move across the moonlight
They shimmer while they lift their arms, like opal, or lit water;
The heaped apples they are eating

Like pebbles on a lake's bed glistening there,
Through many mirrors shown—

He speaks—
" My nightingale,
See how these leaves do hide us!
Their bunched and quilted thickness, since they're clouds, not trees,
Give closer cover than a leaf's thin blades;
But, like boughs, the wind can lift them,
And show us in the flooding light, fixed and still,
The tents we lie in, all our nets for love,
On the wind's lips hanging, like the slaves who watch your eyelids;
For, ashore, we have the clouds like leaves above us,
And, at sea, our sails against the wind's voice hoisted:
We can stay out in the full light, with not a bough to shelter us,
Or lie out in the cold main, a clump of stars,
With all our torches burning."

She did not answer him but looked towards the sea
Choosing among his words, which place she liked best,
The apple in her hand, with its cool rind, persuading her,
For it lay there shimmering in the moonbeams, sharp and chill,
And she thought of all the loaded boughs that sway down in a little wind,
Till the ripest fruit will fall away and on the grass boom loud:
And how she'd climb up higher through the tree's green core
Cooling with her glossy wings the stem, the beating heart of tree,

While she passed by to the topmost leaves,
To those windows giving on the cold, blue air,
" He calls me his nightingale because I'm dark with sun:
My eyes and my raven hair give his fire a shade,
Dark as the night I sing through,
I will lie among the branches like a light in the clouds
For him to find me—"
And, while she thinks of this, he waits and listens
For the music, like a tree of birds, sings out loud
Ringing from the balcony above their heads
As though each instrument sang from a bough,
Its soft throat mingling with the measured music,
Till, in the town below, a trumpet sounds,
Raising its eagle voice above the roofs,
To tell the soldiers of deep midnight.

Still faster did the hours pass, while all else slept
They burnt away like lamps, while the two of them scarce spoke,
So still the air now, with no cloud, no wind,
No music from the gallery—
Moonlight through the lowest branches came
Sloping from the sea's rim, down that wall of water,
In at those windows opening wide and low
Between the branches, where light breaks and falls
Off the leaf's edge tumbling like a spurt of rain,
While it pours, and the straight lines of light show them there.
Out of this bright sea with not a leaf to hide her
The nightingale starts singing now,
Her fiery words said softly for his ear alone,
In gusts and little stabbing jets
To conquer him,
And, as her lips are singing, the dawn wind begins,

Still lower does the light fall till it drinks the sea
Slaking its thirsty throat before it sinks and sleeps:
The silver wings of light are furled,
It hovers for the flight's end in the wind from off the water
And now its throat is touching and its silver plumes are wet,
They flutter in the water but they cannot stay its weight,
And as it sinks in ocean that other nightingale who watches it
Calls for wine to fill her glass and lifts her flower soft hands,
Loosing the pearl that hangs between her breasts,
Like the precious egg of nightingales hid in fruit boughs safe and still,
And she lifts the pearl away from them,
Out from those branches, from their leaves and soft flower petals,
To melt in the red wine like a cloud dissolved in fire—
It lies in the glass while all its beauty leaves it;
As a shell that crumbles under foot
It powders, and its dust is white,
And, now it's only ashes, she will lift it high,
Drinking down this rainbow, since it's bent and broken,
While wind lifts the curtains, and the salt sea smells,
Its wide plain flat and still for those moving tents to pitch upon;
Then thought she:—
" I will have the sails set, and no leaves for cover,
We will lie out in the cold main, a clump of stars
With all our torches burning and the sails to shelter us,
The day we'll spend in travelling till we've lost the land
And through the night we'll drift just where the waves command,
Too rapt by my singing to be careful of the way:

I'll be softer than water and as cool as wind,
Like the dolphin out of the wavecrests I'm as quick as light,
For my voice is like the nightingale, and starlight is no
    gaudier;
Like a silver gliding fish I'll leap,
Or lie quite still if you'll but hold me."

GROUP XIII

Studies on the Black Keys

1. *The Dark of Night*

Come, leave that battlefield, put down your steel,
For night is hushing down the sleepy hills:
Be gentle with your prisoners, the fair haired corn,
Let wind run to cool their wounds till fair haired morning stirs again
To fire the sheaves once more
Before the millstone and the threshing floor.
Now the glitter on great leaves is dead, and stars in distant windows born
Suckle at darkness;
The shawm, the drum of skin, the reed pipe lingering for a fill of breath,
Mingle their music with the singing of thick lips
From ebon faces with black wool of lambs sown for their shading.
While there is this echo on the pipes of wind,
Like the female fashioned from the ribs of man,
Light, a gentle silver light, out of the couch of sun
Climbs into fulness,
Her light, that is an echoed light, throws water on the thirsty sheaves
And turns those fair haired prisoners to a winter touch of snow,
Mocking at summer and the sun's return.

Let ebon limbs, and paler limbs in hue,
Mingle their sweetness at the flower's mouth,
Drinking new life from thick petals of the flowerlike lips,
Before the hoary winter comes and age goes white.

2. *Black Sonnet*

BLACK bodies by the crystal water born,
Cradled on sand and from the hot sun hid,
Lest his bold eye shall burn their infant lid,
On softest palm leaves, smoothed, without a thorn,
Cry for the ebon breast; just as forlorn
Those milk white bodies where the cold winds bid
Snow to fall paler than the milk that slid
Through weak lips. Ebon black, or pale as corn,
They grow and blossom up beneath the sky,
Changing like trees until they stand fullgrown,
A black branch of fire, safe hid and shady,
Or gold hair, sun on leaves, their cool fruit shown.
Men of all races! This Eternity
You have to choose from. Is the trumpet blown?

3. *Black Shepherdess*

BLACK shepherdess, among your lambs
Dwells sweet innocence, like untrod snow,
Their curled spring raiment soiled by everything but sun;
Why is your crisp hair, spun like theirs,
Mantled with darkness?
Were you born in a valley at the back of day
By a wood of starlight, nursed at that camp fire?

Did ghosts from those thickets walk about your land
So the tent of the shepherdess was cumbered with gold armour
Till the hero left your mother and turned back into the glade,
Bright as his armour?
Were you born from that wedlock in a darkened land,
Bred in black innocence from blighted vows,
Mocking the young shepherd on the sleepy hills,
Busy with his charges?
Such parents, like day and night mingling their chequers,
Moved you to ripeness, till your infant hair
Grew woolly like the lambs you tend, but black as fate.
The sun has burnt you, who were born in shade,
Claiming his fatherhood,
For the light on armour and the thicket of wild starlight
Were both but echoes of his ceaseless fire,
That drops through corn or down blue fields of sea
Moving, or it seems to move, and never dying,
But come back like the shepherd on the morning hills,
Sleepy with shadow.

Two Pastoral Poems
(*From the designs of Edward Calvert, the disciple of William Blake*)

1. *The Cyder Feast*

STONE guests, and all the monkish shades,
Here is no canvas for your tragedies;
Gold armoured ghosts their waisted waspish din
Must keep from the apple harvest,

There is no banquet door, no drum unto their gauntlet,
Nor even wattles for our cloud-like lambs
To prison them in cells that are their bread and light;
Such reedy battlements no ghost can shake
Who lives in his own histories to trumpet sound
Walking the long reaches of what once were shores,
Where he paced, but never left, the spongy sand;
And thus our green summer, and the sea lit night
Fired by the moonlight off that window in the world,
Are safe, there is no battery of beaten hopes,
No forlorn feaster in the mirror at our shoulder,
Who, unbidden, like the ghost he is, in dead leaves of summer
Should wait till we joined him;
No walls, no battlements, no haunted woods,
No stair for his feet, and not a door for his plumes to brush:
We are feasting without torches in thick shade of trees.

All day long in light or heavy branches
Did we toil at the virgins whose green sleeves of wind
We lifted and the cloth of leaves in breath of their own blowing
Laid back to loose the silver cords that held them;
Then apple after apple from that tree of bright globes
Fell and we gathered those Ephesian breasts
Till the tree, that living goddess, to dead statue turned
And we left her in the apple wood and moved our ladders
To pluck in green sleeves at other towers of sweetness.
All day among the turrets of that green world of winds
We wandered and hid chambers in the steep stairs found
Where apples, sunny honeycombs, in hidden windows hung,
Which we entered like robbers after bags of gold
And climbed from those window sills too heavy for our ladders.

While the tree into dead statue turned at its cold sister's side.
All day, while we were singing and the summer wind blew sweet,
I heard the swollen mill waters,
They were in our gentle branches like the drums of fate
While they ground their golden prisoners to a white and shameful dust
And the fields, like our apple trees, lay bruised and sore.

2. *Chamber Idyll*

" In time of year
When cherry trees enticing burdens bear,
He that with wreathed legs doth upwards go,
Plucks not alone for those which stand below;
But now and then is seen to pick a few
To please himself as well as all his crew,
Or if from where he is he do espy
An apricock upon a bough thereby
Which overhangs the tree on which he stands,
Climbs up and strives to take it with his hands."

O, stay with me, goatfoot, where the grass is high,
It makes a sweet meadow for your hoofs to tread,
While cherries, lively coals of fire,
But only burning to our eyes,
Hang near us, or are handed from the ladder tower;
Like this,
Soothing grass will hush the animal in you,
And cherries, that are man's delight,
You can feed your mortal soul upon.
O stay with me and talk to me!

But the goat god never spoke, he never risked his immortality;
Often is it so in chamber idylls, and in idle dreams,
Where we speak and are not answered,
Or hear the voice of poetry and say no word ourselves;
Yet he stood at my side among the orchard boughs,
And we lived an hour—an age—in this world beyond my window.
Where is the mortal in this earth that is so infinite,
That moves with me, boundless, and builds before my eyes,
That is prodigal, or bitter, that will give me shores of amber,
Or sharp rocks, the fangs of sea:
Will they die, the changing shadows of this chamber idyll?
For death, where once was life, is not the same as death unborn!
Back from that shore among these orchard trees
I moved among my changes, at the goat god's side,
But kept these dreams among the boughs and never left them.
We lived, all that noon, deep in the cherry shade
Moving each ladder as the climber tired
To change the harvester upon its rungs
And the goat god took his turn with them,
But yet he never spoke to me
And only for the cherries did he move his lips.

Then Midas, the miser, took me back with him,
And we lived, in an instant, where that noon was left
Gilding the ladder foot at each gold tree,
Where he spared no wealth of his
And the climbers, like Hylas and like Ganymede,
Seemed stolen into heaven,
Their wreathed legs, against this cloud of fire,

Stood strong upon the ladders that we moved with them
And they threw the sprigs of flame to us and climbed yet
   further,
Fighting at the cherry heart.

And now to the edges of this magic wood
We came from that slaughter to the last tree's fate,
Where it leaned above a red wall,
The finite, the horizon, to this ghost of Midas,
For he and the goat god only walked the noonday wood
And never could come out of it, for fear I should awake.
His gold against my broken sleep did Midas spend
And for his last breath of safety made the goat god climb,
Hazarding this heaven with his treacherous hooves,
But they held to the ladder rung, and he climbed high
Till he saw, beyond the wall, ripe honeycombs of corn
Cut deep by the reaper who now rested in some shade.
Then he cried, the goat god, like a bear for honey,
And stretched out a hand towards the harvest,
Shaking the tree stem like a bear his bars;
But the corn never came to him, his greedy hand
Reaching for that mirage, fell upon a sunny apricot.
Midas, the miser and the spendthrift, wept,
His men, on their ladders, let the cherries fall
And dropped from the heavens where they worked and sang
To weep with Midas.
These battles broke the dream, and now my chamber idyll
Fades from noon into the night hours,
I wait through these watches with neither apricot nor cherry,
And only little flowers and little wind I hear.
O, may these change into a wood for Midas,
May we work at the cherry trees in a noon that never ends!
My stone sill, chilly with the moon's cold rays,
Darkens with a ghost again, the play begins.

GROUP XIV (July, 1947)

White Rose

I saw someone by the white syringa,
I saw someone under the white syringa tree.
But it comes to this, that there is no one left,
That if I think I saw someone, it was imagination,
For what I never expected to happen, has happened,
And you are dead.

In a few weeks, when the earth wakens,
We could see someone, it matters not whom,
Standing under the white Guelder-rose,
And the ghosts of the castle
Coming out in person.

A young woman wearing a mask,
Riding under the Turkish lilac,
While rain dashes from the white spires
Upon her face and hands.

The white rose bush,
Burning,
Which had stood asleep;
The burning rose tree,
The white rose on fire.

The Mezquita

Coming out of the snow,
I found the court of the mosque
Full of orange trees in blossom;
So about the time there was a death
There was a birth.

It is the Man God of two wars
That has lost its scent and lost its wisdom.

The Lime Avenue

It rained
Upon the tall windows
In the tall old house,
In the morning and in the evening.

What a long morning
Of mystery,
With music not far away,
Looking at the rain;
What a world within a world
In a rainy day!

In midst of it
We walked in the wet garden,
Under the wet limes;
And so the long morning
Wept itself away.

Outside Dunsandle

WHAT a liar
    Was the tinker woman whom we met
Under the long stone wall!
But what a creature of mystery
With her tousled terrible child,
Eating bread,
And her veiled eyes.

She told us the wrong way to go,
Only for a few coppers,
Knowing we should come back again.
She watched, while the boy
With frayed sleeves and groundsel hair
Munched away.

She would have sent us over the edge of the world
For a few pennies,
Far away there out in the west.
I see her in the long rags of rain
Gathering wet sticks
For the turf fire,
Waiting for lost travellers to come by.

The Sick Man

I HAVE never seen a man look so ill
  As the Paper Man of Carrick,
He was waiting there on the quay
Every time we came down to the river.

He was so pale that he looked as though
Fine dust had been blown onto him from head to foot,
So listless that it was a wonder
He could walk as far down as the river.

He was like the ghost of the gaunt warehouse,
Or of the mill that had long ago stopped working;
His body and his fearful clothes
Had the consistency of bleached paper.

And at last I could stand it no longer,
And went up and spoke to him;
Yes, he felt very ill, and had terrible pains in his legs and
    ankles,
He must be dying, I suppose, of some disease of the kidneys.

He was under Dr. Callaghan,
And went to the hospital to see him two days a week:
Next morning, there was no sign of him,
But only a little gust of wind blew out of the warehouse
    door,

Blew out of the sightless door,
And shook the dust into the river.

INDEX OF FIRST LINES

	PAGE
A bed, a chair, a table, and a cupboard	47
A glass gives no sure echo	150
A wall of cactus guards the virgin sound	131
Begin with water	78
Black bodies by the crystal water born	180
Black faces by the crystal water born	173
Black shepherdess, among your lambs	180
Blow your long horn	128
Bohemund, give us Bohemund, and take back time	108
Bread, cheese and wine	20
By the Rio Grande	15
Come, leave that battlefield, put down your steel	179
Coming out of the snow	188
Deep do the letters bite that spell the name	169
"Do the fish still glitter in the waterpool?"	67
For safety, hear this, common mortals!	29
Full moon fruit hanging on the orchard tree	120
Grass, that green fire, is lit	155
Heroes out of music born	100
How even, flat and similar	119
I have never seen a man look so ill	189
If you feel for it pressing back the glossy leaves	146
I lived through the summer while I looked for shade	149
In time of year	183
I saw someone by the white syringa	187
I see no breath upon the window's water	142
It is only this last century that the crack appeared	138
It rained	188
My salamander in a world of flame	143

	PAGE
Oh! how this music throbs and lifts our feet!	125
Open your window. Let the air flow in	141
Our orange wood and lemon glade	148
Pindar asleep beneath the planes	117
Rex Tremendæ Majestatis	71
Ring, gold bell, and the loud sun will laugh	152
River-like, this cold quick wind	123
Shadow, Shadow	156
Shake, stone shades	18
Sigh soft, sigh softly	141
Something of a soldier is each poet	170
Sprechen sie Deutsch? Parlez-vous Francais?	126
Stone guests, and all the monkish shades	181
Sun and rain at work together	145
Tall as a ghost . . . outside . . . the soldier	17
The door grates open. Two wild eyes look out	159
The gold voice of the sunset was most clearly in the air	114
The mere act of talking blew those ashes in our faces	135
The parrot's voice snaps out	116
The prophet from his desert cave	23
These lions, each by a daisy queen	148
These two keep summer in their lips	146
The stars, but prophets call them sons of God	37
The white nightingale is hidden in the branches	121
The wood is one blue flame of love	152
'Tis a pity they are ashes!	135
Tomb	85
You lily beds and lily plains	149
What a liar	189
When the hood of night comes on the land	121
White clouds	94
Wind barked all night just outside	21
Wind, come run to help me	144
Wind is husbandman, the sun's heat carrying	68
Woven from the tangled hair of comets	113